LESSONS IN FARM LIFE
with spiritual applications

by
Nancy Graham

Illustrations by Melissa Graham

Copyright © 2015 Nancy Graham.

All rights reserved. No part of this book may be used or reproduced by
any means, graphic, electronic, or mechanical, including photocopying,
recording, taping or by any information storage retrieval system
without the written permission of the publisher except in the case
of brief quotations embodied in critical articles and reviews.

Scripture quotations are from The Holy Bible, English Standard
Version® (ESV®), copyright © 2001 by Crossway, a publishing ministry
of Good News Publishers. Used by permission. All rights reserved.

Scripture taken from the King James Version of the Bible.

WestBow Press books may be ordered through
booksellers or by contacting:

WestBow Press
A Division of Thomas Nelson & Zondervan
1663 Liberty Drive
Bloomington, IN 47403
www.westbowpress.com
1 (866) 928-1240

Because of the dynamic nature of the Internet, any web addresses or
links contained in this book may have changed since publication and
may no longer be valid. The views expressed in this work are solely those
of the author and do not necessarily reflect the views of the publisher,
and the publisher hereby disclaims any responsibility for them.

Any people depicted in stock imagery provided by Thinkstock are models,
and such images are being used for illustrative purposes only.
Certain stock imagery © Thinkstock.

ISBN: 978-1-4908-8473-8 (sc)
ISBN: 978-1-4908-8474-5 (e)

Library of Congress Control Number: 2015909596

Print information available on the last page.

WestBow Press rev. date: 07/27/2015

Scripture taken from the New King James Version. Copyright 1979, 1980, 1982 by Thomas Nelson, inc. Used by permission. All rights reserved.

Scripture quotations taken from the New American Standard Bible®, Copyright © 1960, 1962, 1963, 1968, 1971, 1972, 1973, 1975, 1977, 1995 by The Lockman Foundation. Used by permission." (www.Lockman.org)

Scriptures taken from the Holy Bible, New International Version®, NIV®. Copyright © 1973, 1978, 1984, 2011 by Biblica, Inc.™ Used by permission of Zondervan. All rights reserved worldwide. www.zondervan.com The "NIV" and "New International Version" are trademarks registered in the United States Patent and Trademark Office by Biblica, Inc.™ All rights reserved.

Introduction

I never really considered myself a writer. In fact, if anything, I thought I would end up more in the artist profession, as that is where my interest lay for several years. I did actually do some painting for various people at one time. However, due to homeschooling and hobby farming, I haven't had time for my painting in recent years. Now that I am left with just one child at home to school, I am finding more time for other pursuits. Perhaps I will return to my painting at some point, but for now I have felt strongly compelled to write these stories, with the addition of some spiritual applications.

I would like to make some acknowledgments in regards to this book to start off with. First and foremost, had it not been for the amazing work of God's Holy Spirit within my life these past few years, I would not have been capable of taking on such a project, nor would I even have had the desire to do so. My intention in writing this book was to have something tangible to pass down to my family; something in writing to attest to the fact that the working of God's Holy Spirit within my life has made a radical difference- not only in the way that I live, but in

vii

the very thoughts that I think. I want my whole focus to be on living for the glory of God and I would love to see evidence of that same desire in each member of our family- and in others as well. God has given me a real love and compassion for those who do not know him in a real way. I know this love comes only from God, for I could not love in the way I do now, nor have a love for the people that I do now in my own strength.

I would be remiss if I neglected to mention a very dear couple by the names of Alex and Betty Graham, who actually planted the seed for the idea of this book several years ago. I'm not sure exactly how many years ago it has been, since the older I get, the faster the years seem to go by. I would however, like to express my appreciation to these dear friends for their interest in the stories that I used to relate to them some time back, as well as their suggestion that I put them into print. I would also like to express my utmost appreciation for their diligence and dedication in reading through, and editing, each and every section of this book. At the time they suggested I write a book, I really never gave it much thought; besides not having the time to take on such a project, I certainly did not feel qualified for the task. However, as I grow and mature in the faith, my desire to write has become more of a passion, because my goal to glorify God in all that I do becomes stronger as I grow in my love for him. I am more and more motivated to be used of God- not only to be an encouragement to my own family members, but to any and all those He would bring me into contact with.

I would also be remiss if I failed to make mention of my dear husband, Rickey- who through our many discussions of God's Word together these past few years has been a tremendous help to me in the writing of this book. I have been amazed at the wisdom and insight God has given of his precious Word to the spouse that He has blessed me with.

I must not neglect to make mention of our son Nick, as well, whose skills in technology I would have been lost without. I could not have made it through all the stages necessary in order to have this book published without his much needed (and much appreciated) help.

I cannot tell how very delighted I was when our daughter, Melissa, in spite of a busy schedule, consented to doing a few illustrations for this book. I am so thankful to God for blessing our only daughter with such talent. I am actually thankful to our entire family; for the interaction of our many relationships with one another, (especially those closest to us) is one of the means God uses for our sanctification, teaching us many lessons we need to learn.

God has certainly been teaching me *so* many lessons these past few years, and I have gained such a peace and contentment through them, that I want to share with you some of those lessons that I have been learning. I hope you enjoy a few chuckles from some of these stories, but more than that, I pray that the Holy Spirit would teach you from the spiritual insights that are included with each one. May you be encouraged to grow and mature in your walk with Christ, our Lord. If you are reading this book and do not know the Lord of whom I speak, I pray that his Holy Spirit would open your eyes to your need for Him, and that you, too, would find a true peace and contentment as you come to experience the wonderful grace and mercy of our loving Lord and Savior, Jesus Christ.

I would like to dedicate this book to all of my family, with special mention of my dear husband, Rickey, who has faithfully prayed *for* me, and displayed *to* me, a true Christ-like love within his life.

Contents

1	Milk to Meat	1
2	Ignorance is not Bliss	13
3	Pride Before a Call	27
4	Travelling On	39
5	Out of Sight Out of Mind	49
6	Stubborn and Stiff-necked	58
7	Follow the Leader	73
8	Restraints and Restrictions	80
9	Doing Your Duty	89
10	Submission and Authority	98
11	Denying Self	110
12	Is the Grass Really Greener?	116
13	Bawling for Babies	127
14	Be on Your Guard	136
15	Equipped for the Task	151
16	Don't Give Up!	169
17	To Be.. Or Not to Be..	184
18	Pursuing Presumptions	195
19	Fickle, Fleeting, Or.. Forever!	213

xiii

| 20 | Showing His Sovereignty | 230 |
| 21 | Come to the Call... | 249 |

Autobiographical Note	259
List of Books for Recommended Reading	267
Postscript	269

1

Milk to Meat

Ephesians 4:11-16

My husband and I were quite excited about getting into some hobby farming when we acquired a huge farm house and barn in the Lake-ville area several years ago. Among some of the first animals we acquired were two Jersey cows. One of them had been bred with a Jersey bull and the other with a Blond d' Aquitaine. We were pleased to have a healthy little purebred heifer from the one cow and even happier to have quite a size-able calf from the one bred to the d' Aquitaine. The little one we named Bambi, as she looked just like a little fawn. The second calf was also a heifer, but quite a size larger. This one we called Taffy, because of her color. They both became quite the pets. Of course as the years went by and we acquired more wisdom and experience in our hobby farming, we did come to realize it isn't such a good idea to make pets

Milk to Meat

of your livestock. Actually we came to realize that fairly early in Taffy's case. She had become a great favorite and we really made quite a lot of her, too much in fact. Going out to the barn to play with Taffy became a favorite pasttime. She just seemed so full of personality, and so- I'm afraid we treated her more as another pet, rather than part of our livestock.

It was fine and good to rub her head and romp around with her when she was little. However, as she got bigger- and bigger she did get- she seemed totally unaware that she should be growing out of this stage. She still wanted to romp, play, and push, even as she passed seven- eight- nine months old. By the time she was a year old we knew we had gotten ourselves into a bit of a quandary. It had in fact got to the stage when it was quite dangerous to go out into the pasture with her unless we were to take a stick along for protection, just in case. If she saw one of us coming, she would run over tossing her head back and forth and expecting attention. After feeling the butt of that hard head against our side, or from behind a few times, we didn't get caught off-guard very often. It wasn't that our Taffy had turned nasty, but that she just didn't know her own strength, or realize she had gotten too big for that sort of nonsense. Finally, we sold her to another farmer, and after losing her 'playmates,' she did settle down, turning out to be an excellent cow and very good mother. How pleased we were to learn that she had eventually 'grown up' after all.

Lessons in Farm Life

Thinking back on this episode in our early farming days made me think of the importance of growth in our own lives. Just as we need to feed and nourish our bodies physically with healthy foods in order to promote good physical health, so also do we need to feed our souls with the nourishment of God's Word in order to promote good spiritual health. Some Christians seem to grow and mature spiritually at a much faster rate than others. Do we ever stop and ask ourselves why this is? I believe one of the reasons that some mature so slowly is due to the fact that they seem to be content to remain in the infant stage of their faith. We should not be satisfied to remain as infants or even toddlers in the faith. It is important that we grow and mature. As infants grow and mature physically we need to wean them off milk and gradually work them into eating solid foods. If we continue to feed them milk, their bodies are not going to grow as they would if given the proper nourishment. They will cry for lack of food and become weak and malnourished. So, we too, need to get off the milk and into the meat of God's word, not being content to just absorb the basics of the Christian doctrine, but desiring to consume the full meat of the word. In 1 Corinthians 3:1-3 Paul tells the church *"...I, brothers, could not address you as spiritual people, but as people of the flesh, as infants in Christ. I fed you with milk, not solid food, for you were not ready for it And even now you are not yet ready, for you are still in the flesh. For while there is jealousy and strife among you, are you not of the flesh and behaving only in a human way?"* If the Corinthians

3

Milk to Meat

were truly Christians, their behavior failed to testify to that fact, so Paul had to treat the people as ones with very little spiritual understanding. I pray we do not fall in this category as well.

We need to be acting in such a way as to show evidence of the Holy Spirit's work within our lives. Evidence of spiritual maturity in our lives can be found in the way we handle difficult situations. Do we display evidence of the fruit of the Spirit in our lives in times of testing? For instance, how would we react to the breaking of a window or perhaps an old family heirloom, by one of our children? Would we be overly upset by the carelessness of our child, or at the loss of a treasured item? Or would we use the situation as a valuable teaching opportunity, helping our child to realize the insignificance of material things, and at the same time, teaching him to take responsibility for his own actions? Would we show patience and forgiveness, thereby teaching him (or her) how important it is to be patient and forgiving when he has to deal with someone who does something against him, *"And we urge you, brothers, admonish the idle, encourage the fainthearted, help the weak, be patient with them all" (1 Thessalonians 5:14)?*

I believe another reason why some seem to mature much more slowly than others is that they have not been taken in and discipled as they should be. It is so important for new believers to have help and instruction, to be able to ask questions and discuss the word of God with at least one other person who is more knowledgeable of God's word, or within a group of believers within a church

Lessons in Farm Life

family. We should not take for granted that they will soak up God's word and understand all that they read and hear, without the encouragement and clarification of those who are more mature in the faith. It is imperative for them to be taught who God is and what He requires of us. It is probable that they are either in school or in the workplace for at least five days a week, surrounded for the most part by ungodly influences, and thus it would be extremely difficult to counteract all this by merely listening to one or two sermons once a week. Nowadays, few churches even offer two worship services on the Lord's Day, and even if they did- this would not be enough for new Christians to gain all they need to get them through the following week. Every new believer needs to be encouraged to nourish their soul for their spiritual good, as they must nourish their body for their physical good- in order to grow and mature in the faith. Those who are mature in the faith should be ministering to those who are new or immature in the faith, *"We who are strong have an obligation to bear with the failings of the weak, and not to please ourselves. Let each of us please his neighbor for his good, to build him up" (Romans 15:1-2). "And He gave the apostles, the prophets, the evangelists, the pastors and teachers, to equip the saints for the work of ministry, for building up the body of Christ, until we all attain to the unity of the faith and of the knowledge of the Son of God, to mature manhood, to the measure of the stature of the fullness of Christ, so that we may no longer be children, tossed to and fro by the waves and carried about by every wind of doctrine, by human cunning, by craftiness in*

Milk to Meat

deceitful schemes. Rather, speaking the truth in love, we are to grow up in every way into him who is the head, into Christ, from whom the whole body, joined and held together by every joint with which it is equipped, when each part is working properly, makes the body grow so that it builds itself up in love" (*Ephesians 4:11-16*).

I firmly believe that another reason why some of us fail to mature as quickly as others in the faith is due to a failure to receive good sound teaching. I think there are many believers out there who truly desire to grow in the faith, but due to years of attendance in churches where the pastor has failed to teach the whole counsel of God they are missing out on a lot of good solid teaching that could have a drastic effect on the way they live their lives. They are just being spoon fed with milk, being deprived of the meat of God's word. They need to be encouraged to really grow and mature in the wisdom and knowledge of our Lord.

Unfortunately, there are pastors out there who seem not to understand or take seriously the tremendous responsibility that is theirs, as shepherds of the flock of God, *"So I exhort the elders among you, as a fellow elder and a witness of the sufferings of Christ, … shepherd the flock of God that is among you, exercising oversight, not under compulsion, but willingly, as God would have you; not for shameful gain, but eagerly, not domineering over those in your charge, but being examples to the flock"* (*1 Peter 5:1-3*).

If the pastor himself is not mature in the faith, it is unlikely that his congregation will grow and mature past

Lessons in Farm Life

his own level, *"A disciple is not above his teacher, but everyone when he is fully trained will be like his teacher" (Luke 6:40).* Therefore if those within the congregation are not diligent in studying their Bibles and praying for wisdom and discernment in understanding what they read, then they will probably fail to see what is lacking in the teaching they do receive, *"If any of you lacks wisdom, let him ask God, who gives to all without reproach, and it will be given him. But let him ask in faith, with no doubting, for the one who doubts is like a wave of the sea that is driven and tossed by the wind" (James 1:5).* The wisdom that is spoken of here is not an earthly wisdom, *"For the wisdom of this world is folly with God" (1 Corinthians 3:19),* but it is referring to the wisdom that comes from God, the fear of the Lord; The kind of wisdom that helps us to understand God's word and apply it to our lives. This is the kind of wisdom we need to be asking for, *"Behold **the fear of the Lord, that is wisdom**, and **to turn away from evil is understanding**" (Job 28:28). "Who is wise and understanding among you? By his good conduct let him show his works in the meekness of wisdom" (James 3:13). "… the wisdom from above is first pure, then peaceable, gentle, open to reason, full of mercy and good fruits, impartial and sincere. And a harvest of righteousness is sown in peace by those who make peace" (James 3:17–18).* These verses would indicate that the sowing of wisdom in one's life will reap a bountiful harvest of righteousness.

If we fail to go on to maturity in Christ, we will miss out on so many blessings. For when we are faithfully reading and studying His word, looking to Him each day

Milk to Meat

for the grace we need to get through it, we will grow and mature in the faith and bear much fruit. As we mature in the faith, we will be entrusted with more and more responsibilities. A very clear example of this can be seen in David. As a shepherd boy, he faithfully trusted in God to look after him. When he was faced with wild animals while tending his sheep, he fought them off. Being faithful in this responsibility, he is later entrusted to fight the mighty Goliath, confident in God's help again, *"The Lord who delivered me from the paw of the lion and from the paw of the bear will deliver me from the hand of this Philistine" (1 Samuel 17:37).*

David was just a youth at this time and Goliath was a giant. Was David intimidated by this huge man? No! He had complete confidence that God would deliver Goliath into his hands. We are told how this brave young man called out to the defiant Philistine, *"You come to me with a sword and with a spear and with a javelin, but I come to you in the name of the Lord of hosts, the God of the armies of Israel, whom you have defied. This day the Lord will deliver you into my hand, and I will strike you down.... that all this assembly may know that the Lord saves not with sword and spear. For the battle is the Lord's, and he will give you into our hand" (1 Samuel 17: 45–47).*

It must have been a ridiculous- looking sight. On the one side we have the huge Goliath, standing over 9 feet tall, fully equipped with all kinds of armor, a huge spear and javelin; with helmet in place. He must have been quite a fearsome looking candidate. On the other side, we have

Lessons in Farm Life

this ruddy looking young fellow stepping confidently over to challenge Goliath, toting a pretty insignificant looking slingshot with 5 little stones with which to tackle him. David was not afraid of his opponent, and I would be confident in saying that Goliath was not likely the least bit afraid of *his* opponent either, but he should have been, considering David's confident assertions in God's power. God took a seemingly weak young man, in comparison, and gave him the victory over a mighty warrior, a giant of a man such as Goliath, *"For consider your calling, brothers; not many of you were wise according to worldly standards, not many were of noble birth.* **But God chose the foolish in the world to shame the wise; God chose what is weak in the world to shame the strong;** *God chose what is low and despised in the world, even things that are not, to bring to nothing things that are, so that no human being might boast in the presence of God. He is the source of your life in Christ Jesus, whom God made our wisdom and our righteousness and sanctification and redemption. Therefore, as it is written, Let the one who boasts, boast in the Lord" (1 Corinthians 1: 26-30).* Let us also be boasters of God and not ourselves, as David was.

David was a keeper of sheep, he fulfilled his responsibilities faithfully and without fear. When all the other Israelite soldiers, Saul included, were too afraid to fight Goliath, God gave David the privilege and responsibility to take on this tremendous task, *"One who is faithful in a very little is also faithful in much...If then you*

Milk to Meat

have not been faithful in the unrighteous wealth, who will entrust to you the true riches" (Luke16:10-11)?

If we stop and consider; it really wasn't such an impossible situation for this young man to go up against someone nearly twice his size; for David had the creator and ruler of the universe on his side; the almighty, all powerful God of heaven and earth. He put his complete trust in his Almighty God for the victory over this 'seemingly' impossible task. As David had confidently affirmed, God did deliver Goliath into his hand. Nothing is impossible with God; and David was not negligent in giving God all the glory for his victory. We need to remember that when we are faced with our own Goliaths; if we are in Christ, we have the Almighty, Sovereign Creator and ruler of the whole universe on our side. And when He gives us the victory, we need to remember to give Him the glory.

In *Hebrews 5:12-14* we find another exhortation that focuses on the failure to go on to maturity, *"For though by this time you ought to be teachers, you need someone to teach you again the basic principles of the oracles of God. You need milk not solid food, for everyone who lives on milk is unskilled in the word of righteousness, since he is a child. But **solid food is for the mature, for those who have their powers of discernment trained by constant practice to distinguish good from evil.**"* This kind of maturity is evidence of a spiritual discernment that comes from consistent obedience to God's will. In *Philippians 1:9-11* we find Paul encouraging the people, *"And it is my prayer that your love may abound more and more*

Lessons in Farm Life

with knowledge and all discernment, so that you may approve what is excellent, and so be pure and blameless for the day of Christ, filled with the fruit of righteousness that comes through Jesus Christ, to the glory and praise of God."

We must determine not just to be hearers of God's word, but to be doers of it as well. Many times we may sit under the teaching of God's word, hearing it and yet not really listening to it. We may go home and forget what we have heard, not even bothering to attempt to apply it to our lives, *"But be doers of the word, and not hearers only, deceiving yourselves. For if anyone is a hearer of the word and not a doer, he is like a man who looks intently at his natural face in a mirror. For he looks at himself and goes away and at once forgets what he was like. But the one who looks into the perfect law, the law of liberty, and perseveres, being no hearer who forgets but a doer who acts, he will be blessed in his doing"* *(James 1:22-25)*. God's written law upon our hearts sets us free from our slavery to sin. This does not mean we will not sin, but rather sin will not have the hold over us it once did, *"Jesus answered them, Truly, truly, I say to you, everyone who commits sin is a slave to sin. The slave does not remain in the house forever, the son remains forever. So, if the Son sets you free, you will be free indeed" (John 8:34-36).* True freedom is to be given the desire to serve God. It is only due to the grace of God and through the working of His Holy Spirit within our lives freeing us from that sin that we are able to be victorious. We must make a conscious effort to truly listen to God's word and apply it to our lives, being obedient to what God is teaching us,

11

Milk to Meat

realizing that we have been made free from sin and alive to righteousness, *"For it is not the hearers of the law who are righteous before God, but the doers of the law who will be justified" (Romans 2:13)*. Obedience to God's word is a definite sign of maturity in a believer's life.

May we all as believers be encouraged to seek the wisdom that comes from above. Paul's prayer to the Ephesians was that, *"the God of our Lord Jesus Christ, the Father of glory, may give you a spirit of wisdom and of revelation in the knowledge of Him, having the eyes of your hearts enlightened, that you may know what is the hope to which He has called you," (Ephesians 1:17-18)*. My sincere prayer is that He would give each one of us a desire to get into the meat of God's word; that our ears would be open, and hearts ready and willing to act upon the truths that we hear and read, that we would all go on to maturity in Christ.

2

Ignorance is not Bliss

2 Corinthians 13:5

Several years ago when we were no more than novices in our hobby farm exploits, we decided to add a sheep to our list of farm animals. Of course we knew nothing about sheep, but how hard could it be to raise a few? Well, we soon found out how hard it could be when you hadn't done any previous study on the subject. As it turned out for these ignorant sheep farmers the first sheep we bought was due to have her lamb in January. I remember thinking what an awful time of year to have a lamb come due. We had a barn with a few pens in it, but it was not by any means warm. Well, we named our sheep, Maggie, and kept a close watch as her time drew near. Then, as any good sheep farmer would have done in the absence of a

Ignorance is not Bliss

heated barn, we fixed up a pen with a heat light in the unfinished part of our basement, which happened to be directly below our living room.

There was a fair bit of snow that year, so the day that Maggie had her wee lamb, one of our sons was enlisted to maneuver her onto a sled (not an easy task) to bring her up to the house. He actually had to wrestle her onto her back and tie her legs to keep them from flailing all over as she refused to wade through the snow, even for her baby. I'm sure poor Maggie's thoughts, if she'd had any at the time, would have been quite unprintable as she lay hogtied on that bright orange sled, being tugged up to the house through the snow. We actually kept that silly sheep and her baby in the basement until the weather warmed up. You can imagine the surprised looks on people's faces when they came to visit and all of a sudden they would hear the bleating of a sheep beneath their feet. It was really quite amusing, and very entertaining for many friends, who were quite enthralled with the idea of being able to see some real farm animals without having to go out into the cold to do so. Of course we did eventually discover that all we really had to do for our wee lambs when they were born in the winter months, was to bring them inside long enough to dry them off and warm them up, then put them back out with their moms in the barn, where they both belonged.

Thinking back on some of the foolish things we did through our ignorance and neglect as novice hobby farmers made me think about the responsibility we have

14

Lessons in Farm Life

as Christians to be knowledgeable about God's word and to have a right understanding of it in order to apply it appropriately to our lives. It really wasn't that important for us ever to become serious and experienced sheep farmers; which, by the way, and not surprisingly, we did not. However, it is very important we take seriously our claim to be a Christian and that we realize the responsibility that is ours in making this claim; to be a true follower of Christ; one who should exhibit Christ-like qualities in and through his or her life. If we are to be true followers of Christ, we don't want to be guilty of trying to live our Christian lives in ignorance of the many biblical principles that we should be applying to them. If we are to call ourselves Christians, we need to know exactly what a Christian is, how one should act and react, and what kind of qualities we should be displaying in our lives. Yet we must also be careful not to fall into the trap of the Pharisees by listing umpteen dozen rules and regulations to follow and so end up living lives that are essentially very legalistic and yet thinking ourselves to be very righteous and holy.

It seems as if so many of us who call ourselves Christians are living our lives with just a head knowledge of what a Christian should be like, and yet that knowledge seems to contain itself in our brain and does not really reach our hearts, where it can really make a noticeable difference in our lives. We can compare this difference to the composing of a song. The lyrics can be all written out and even memorized. However, until those lyrics are

15

Ignorance is not Bliss

actually put to music, the song is really of very little effect. We need not only an intellectual understanding of the scriptures, but a true 'living it out in our lives' kind of understanding. I'm talking about living a life that displays the fruit of the Spirit. Of course, this can only happen if we have God's holy Spirit living within us. This should be evident in the fruit we display, *"But the fruit of the Spirit is love, joy, peace, patience, kindness, gentleness, self-control..." (Galatians 5:22).* We need to be living a life that is striving after holiness, one that is living in this world, but not conforming to it.

In the book of Revelation, John was instructed to write these words to the church in Laodicea; *"I know your works: you are neither cold nor hot. Would that you were cold or hot! So, because you are lukewarm, and neither hot nor cold, I will spit you out of my mouth" (Revelation 3: 15-16).* If we are outside on a bitter cold day, would we come inside to make ourselves a lukewarm drink? Of course not, we would want a nice hot drink, something to soothe us and warm our insides, just as we would look for a cold refreshing drink on a scorching hot day. Both the hot or cold drink would help to satisfy our need at the time. Similarly, if we were hot and thirsty from a hard day's work in the sun, we would not want to come in to have a lukewarm drink offered to us. We likely would spew it out of our mouths, for it certainly would not satisfy our longing for something cold and refreshing. It would be most unpleasant, just as a lukewarm drink on a bitter cold day would not satisfy our longing for something hot. This

Lessons in Farm Life

is the analogy that is used here. God is saying we need to be hot or cold, not lukewarm, for to be lukewarm is to be of very little effect, unsatisfying, not beneficial.

Sadly, there are many of us who call ourselves Christians in this day and age who are really of no more effect than a lukewarm drink on a hot summer's day. We are not noticeably different from your average Joe who lives a fairly moral life and does not see his need for Christ. So many times we hear the excuse that "the church is full of hypocrites" being used by non-Christians as their reason for not attending. Unfortunately, in some cases this may be true. There very well may *be* hypocrites in our churches, so we had better be certain we are not included among them. We must keep examining ourselves to see if our lifestyle actually fits with our profession of faith, *"Examine yourselves, to see whether you are in the faith. Test yourselves. Or do you not realize this about yourselves, that Jesus Christ is in you- unless indeed you fail to meet the test?" (2 Corinthians 13:5).* How do we examine ourselves? We do so in the light of God's Word, *"Whoever has my commandments and keeps them, he it is who loves me." (John 14:21)* And in verse 24, *"Whoever does not love me does not keep my words"(John 14:21).* See also 2 Peter 1:3-10.

There should be evidence of our salvation in the outworking of our lives. We cannot sit back with the false notion that we have no responsibilities concerning our salvation. The kind of thinking that says, 'Since I can do nothing to earn my salvation, all I really need to do is believe in God and I can rest easy knowing that I will

Ignorance is not Bliss

make it to heaven' is a dangerous kind of thinking, *"Not everyone who says to me, Lord, Lord, will enter the kingdom of heaven, but the one who does the will of my Father who is in heaven" (Matthew 7:21).*

We also need to realize that we are totally unable to live a good enough life to earn our way into heaven. There is absolutely nothing we can do to earn our salvation, *"On that day many will say to me, Lord, Lord, did we not prophesy in your name, and cast out demons in your name, and do many mighty works in your name? And then I will declare to them, I never knew you; depart from me, you workers of lawlessness" (Matthew 7:22-23).* We, as Christians, need to realize that the grounds of our salvation is based on God's grace in sending His Son to pay the penalty for our sin, and the faith we have been given, not on anything that we have done or ever could do, *"For by grace you have been saved through faith. And this is not your own doing; it is the gift of God, not a result of works, so that no one may boast" (Ephesians 2:8-9).* We must realize that apart from Christ, our good deeds count for nothing, *"Abide in me and I in you. As the branch cannot bear fruit by itself, unless it abides in the vine, neither can you, unless you abide in me. I am the vine, you are the branches. Whoever abides in me and I in him, he it is that bears much fruit, for apart from me you can do nothing" (John 15:5).*

It is true that we can do nothing to earn our salvation and we do need to rest in what Jesus has done. However, we also need to realize that we have the responsibility to be working out our salvation, understanding that faith

Lessons in Farm Life

without works is dead, *"But someone will say, 'You have faith and I have works. Show me your faith apart from your works, and I will show you my faith by my works. You believe that God is one; you do well. Even the demons believe-and shudder! Do you want to be shown, you foolish person, that faith apart from works is useless? Was not Abraham our father justified by works when he offered up his son Isaac on the altar? You see that faith was active along with his works;" (James 2:18-22). "Therefore, my beloved, as you have always obeyed, so now, not only as in my presence but much more in my absence, work out your own salvation with fear and trembling, for it is God who works in you, both to will and to work for his good pleasure" (Philippians 2:12-13).* We must understand our responsibility to act in obedience to God's commands, realizing apart from God's grace, we would not desire nor have the ability to obey those commands. We are to act- understanding God is really the One working.

We must not be ignorant of the many biblical principles in God's word. We are responsible to keep God's laws and we cannot use the excuse that 'we didn't know' or we forgot about that instruction, when we mess up and then suffer the consequences for our disobedience. We can look at David's life to see a clear illustration of this. In 2 Samuel chapter 6, we read the account of David and his men bringing the ark of God out of the house of Abinidab. They had the ark on a new cart being driven by oxen. When the oxen stumbled and Uzzah puts out his hand to steady the ark, God strikes him dead. David is angry and afraid to bring the ark into the city. Why

19

Ignorance is not Bliss

did Uzzah die; wasn't he doing a good thing in steadying the ark? Why did this have to happen? It was because David neglected to follow God's instructions. The reason for David's negligence is irrelevant to the fact that he did not follow the proper guidelines according to God's instructions, and as a result, not only he suffered the consequences, but Uzzah did as well.

We cannot put the total blame on David for Uzzah's death, however. Uzzah should have known the ark, which signified God's presence, was holy and not to be touched. When the ark was returned to Israel by the Philistines some of the men of Beth-shemesh looked upon it and were struck down as a result; *"And he struck some of the men of Beth-shemesh, because they looked upon the ark of the Lord. He struck seventy men of them, and the people mourned because the Lord had struck the people with a great blow" (1 Samuel 6:19).* We must remember that we serve an unchanging God, He is the same today as He was back in David's day. He does not allow sin to go unpunished. We also will suffer the consequences if we neglect to follow His commands, so we must be diligent in the study of God's word.

We can read that David did realize the repercussions of his actions and corrected them later on, *"Consecrate yourselves, you and your brothers, so that you may bring up the ark of the Lord, the God of Israel, to the place that I have prepared for it. Because you did not carry it the first time, the Lord our God broke out against us, because we did not seek him according to the rule. "So the priests and the Levites consecrated*

20

Lessons in Farm Life

themselves to bring up the ark of the Lord, the God of Israel. And the Levites carried the ark of God on their shoulders with the poles, as Moses had commanded according to the word of the Lord" (1 Chronicles 15:12-15); "You shall make poles of acacia wood and overlay them with gold. And you shall put the poles into the rings on the sides of the ark to carry the ark by them. The poles shall remain in the rings of the ark; they shall not be taken from it" (Exodus 25:13-15). David had learned his lesson and I pray we will learn ours as well. Reading, studying, knowing and obeying God's word is of utmost importance.

Here is another clear example, using David again. Poor David. It will really seem as if I am picking on him before this book is through, for he is used to demonstrate 'how not to do things' so many times. And yet, we know that David was 'a man after God's own heart'; (1 Samuel 13:14). He was a man who fully trusted in his God, as we have already seen illustrated in the story of Goliath, and we can find many other illustrations showing David's total confidence and trust in the Lord. He certainly didn't live an exemplary lifestyle, for he failed many times: Adultery, murder, and failure in the rearing of his children are obvious illustrations that we are told about, yet, there is one area he did not fail in, and that was in his trust in an Almighty Sovereign God who he believed time and again would give him victory over his battles. That is why I do not believe (after discussing it with my husband) that the reason for David's punishment in his giving of the census (found in second Samuel chapter 24) was due to his lack

21

Ignorance is not Bliss

of trust in God to deliver him from his enemies, but **again** to his neglect to follow God's instructions, *"The Lord said to Moses, When you take the census of the people of Israel, then each shall give a ransom for his life to the Lord when you number them, **that there be no plague among them when you number them**. Each one who is numbered in the census shall give this: half a shekel according to the shekel of the sanctuary (the shekel is twenty gerahs), half a shekel as an offering to the Lord. Everyone who is numbered in the census, from twenty years old and upward, shall give the Lord's offering. The rich shall not give more, and the poor shall not give less, than the half shekel, when you give the Lord's offering to make atonement for your lives. You shall take the atonement money from the people of Israel and shall give it for the service of the tent of meeting, that it may bring the people of Israel to remembrance before the Lord, so as to make atonement for your lives" (Exodus 30:11-16).* We cannot find any inference in 2 Samuel to indicate that David followed these instructions, yet when he is given three choices of punishment for his sin; (1) three years of famine, (2) three months of being pursued by his enemies, or (3) three days of pestilence; this is his response; *"I am in great distress. Let us fall into the hand of the Lord, for his mercy is great; but let me not fall into the hand of man" (2 Samuel 24:14).* This is a man who would put his faith and trust in God over man in every instance. If only we, as God's people today would show such an unfailing trust in our Sovereign Lord. The kind of impact we would have as Christians with such a David- like display of trust in our mighty God would

Lessons in Farm Life

be phenomenal. A trust like this can only come from a right understanding of who God is; and the only way we can find this out is by the revelation of his Holy Spirit-. through the study of His word.

So many people seem to have the idea that theology, which is the study of God, is not important. As long as we love the Lord, that's all that matters. Yet, Jesus says if you love me you will keep my words, and if you do not love me you will not keep my words. So, how can we in all sincerity say that we love the Lord and yet at the same time see no need to read and study His word (so that we might keep it) which is exactly the way in which He says we show our love for Him? It's like saying we love our husbands yet don't really care to know much about them. We need to know their likes and dislikes so that we will be better able to please them. For example, if you knew your husband absolutely detested baked beans, it would not be very appropriate for you to serve him a meal of baked beans in order to show your love for him. In this same line of thought we must study God's Word as a display of our love for him that we might follow his commands and know what is pleasing and what is displeasing to Him. We want to be able to do what is pleasing and avoid what is displeasing to our Lord. Our actions must be consistent with our profession.

What do we find ourselves as Christians, most often, discussing together? How often do we really talk about the things of the Lord when we gather with our families and friends who also profess His name? Do we find

Ignorance is not Bliss

ourselves more often discussing the weather, our cars, homes, latest purchases... in other words, worldly things? Not that there is never a time or place to discuss such things, but does it not make sense that we spend more time discussing the things that are of most importance to us? As Christians, should we not then, find ourselves discussing spiritual matters more often than anything else? In John Bowers book, <u>Portrait of a Soldier</u>, he writes of Thomas Jackson, alias 'Stonewall'. This famous general who served during the Civil War, also served as a Presbyterian deacon and was well known for his devotion to God. Bowers reports that Jackson's first wife had been from a 'devoutly Christian family.' He relates that Jackson held religious discussions with Dr. Junkin, (who would have been his father-in-law), and also his wife's two brothers. "Hour after hour in the parlor they mulled over theology." It seems clear that spiritual matters were of most importance to that family of long ago. What do the discussions that we hold around our tables or in our living rooms show to be of most importance within our families today? Are we too caught up with the things of this world... in other words, are we 'too earthly minded to be of any heavenly good?'

It is imperative that we study His Word in order to live faithful consistent Christian lives, learning all that God requires of us, and it is important that we discuss God's word within our families as well. In Deuteronomy 10:12, we read, "*...what does the Lord your God require of you, but to fear the Lord your God, to walk in all His ways,*

Lessons in Farm Life

to love Him, to serve the Lord your God with all your heart and with all your soul, and to keep the commandments and statutes of the Lord, ..." He gives us these commandments for our good and for the protection, not only of ourselves, but also of the generations to follow, *"Oh, that they had such a mind as this always, to fear me and to keep all my commandments, that it might go well with them and with their descendants forever" (Deuteronomy 5:29)!* How it must grieve our heavenly Father when we willfully disobey Him, incurring much pain not only on ourselves, but on those who are close to us as well.

If we are reading and studying as we should be, then when temptation comes our way, as it will, the Holy Spirit will convict us and we will be able to bring to mind verses of scripture that will help steer us away from that temptation, *"I have stored up your word in my heart, that I might not sin against you" (Psalm 119:11).* Not only our words and our actions should show that our focus is on doing God's will, but even our thoughts should reflect that intent, for our Lord knows even the thoughts that we think, *"For the weapons of our warfare are not of the flesh but have divine power to destroy strongholds. We destroy arguments and every lofty opinion raised against the knowledge of God, and take every thought captive to obey Christ," (2 Corinthians 10:4-5). "He who teaches man knowledge- the Lord- knows the thoughts of man,..." (Psalm 94:11).* The realization that our God knows our every thought is a sobering thing. Not only can we grieve the Holy Spirit through our words and our actions, we can also grieve him with our thoughts,

25

Ignorance is not Bliss

so let us be careful to 'take every thought captive' to the obedience of our Lord.

In Psalm 119:105 we read, *"Your word is a lamp to my feet and a light to my path."* The many things God reveals to us in His word will provide us with the insight we need to direct our steps so we will not stumble in the darkness. How many of us would want to run down to the basement in search of a tool in a house void of light without the aid of a flashlight? It would be pretty silly would it not, especially if you knew exactly where to find one. Your search would be much more fruitful with the shedding of light to your path, not to mention a lot less dangerous.

It is the same with God's word. Why would we even attempt to live in this dark world of sin as Christians without the aid of God's word shedding light to our path and directing us how to live in a way that would help to keep us from stumbling? We need to be knowledgeable of God's word and praying for a right understanding of it, *"Study to show thyself approved unto God, a workman that needs not to be ashamed, rightly dividing the word of truth"* *(2 Timothy 2:15).*

We, as Christians, surely do have a tremendous task in fulfilling the role that God has called us to. Let us not be ignorant of our calling and the many responsibilities our Lord has entrusted to each one of us.

3

Pride Before a Call

Proverbs 16:18

Thinking back over the Jerseys we used to own, I will always remember one with a certain amount of pride. Her name was Annabelle and I was quite proud to say that I could call her name with complete confidence, knowing she would come at the sound of my voice. There are two particular incidents that are etched upon my mind when I think of this beautiful bossy. These incidents both took place at our Lakeville farm. The first happened when a fellow showed up to look at a horse trailer we had for sale at that time. I don't remember who the man was or anything much about him other than the fact that he had an interest in Jerseys, for when he found out we owned one, I knew I had piqued his interest. He asked

Pride Before a Call

where she was for she was not visible within the fenced in area that he could see. I replied she must be out in the back pasture. He seemed disappointed, as if thinking she must be too far away to bother trying to bring in. I replied nonchalantly that I could give her a call if he liked. His disappointment turned to surprise, "You can do that?" He asked incredulously. "Sure," was my confident answer. I then cupped my hands over my mouth ready to give a holler, "ANNABELLE, OH, ANNABELLE!" We didn't have to wait too long before we heard the sound of a tinkling bell and there appeared my beautiful brown bovine. "That's the way it should be done," said he emphatically. I could tell he was obviously impressed. I heartily agreed, feeling a wee bit puffed up with pride, (well, maybe more than just a wee bit). Anyway, not too long after this incident, I was very grateful for this ability to call my obliging bossy by name knowing she would quickly appear at the sound of my voice. However, my feelings at that time were anything but proud.

It was a rather foggy morning and I had just received a not so pleasant phone call from our neighbor across the road. Now this lady was a most genial sort, always very friendly in any contact I had had with her previously. However, I could not help detecting the sound of annoyance in her voice, with a distinct undertone of anger. It seemed that my lovely lass, Annabelle, had found her way out of the fence and over to my neighbor's flower garden. She had been munching on her daffodils, lilies or some such flowers. I can't recall exactly which kind

28

Lessons in Farm Life

they were. My only recollection of that incident was the sound of annoyance in my neighbor's tone of voice and the dismay I felt for my beautiful bossy being the cause of it. I apologized most profusely and did my best to appease her. She was quite understanding and even willing to forgive all if I would just see to it- that it not happen again. I assured her I would do my utmost best to see that it not happen again. However, one cannot make solemn oaths in a matter where cows and fences are concerned. So, having hung up the phone I stepped outside and cupping my hands over my mouth gave a holler once again. "ANNABELLE, OH, ANNABELLE," and to my relief, but not surprise, my beautiful but naughty bossy appeared out of the fog. I praised her for coming, scolded her for leaving and put her back into the fence. After being satisfied at having repaired her escape route I then returned to my neglected chores.

Recalling these incidents would certainly bring to mind the old familiar Proverb; "Pride goes before a fall." Or more accurately put; *"Pride goes before destruction and a haughty spirit before a fall" (Proverbs 16:18).* There are great lessons to be learned in the many scripture accounts that can be found of the pride and downfall of various kings.

In the 20th chapter of 2 Kings we read the account of Hezekiah, who was king of Judah at that time. Hezekiah does a foolish thing because of his pride and the ensuing results prove to be disastrous for his kingdom. The King of Babylon had sent envoys with letters and a present to Hezekiah after learning of his illness. Hezekiah welcomes

Pride Before a Call

these Babylonians and naively shows them all his treasure house. In fact everything that was found in his storehouses Hezekiah proudly displays, hoping to impress them with his nation's wealth and power and perhaps even encourage a treaty with Babylon. However, Hezekiah does not take into account that the same treasures that may induce a treaty with the Babylonians might also incite an invasion.

The Lord had graciously healed Hezekiah of his deathly illness, yet instead of reacting in humility he became proud, *"But Hezekiah did not make return according to the benefit done to him, for his heart was proud. Therefore wrath came upon him and Judah and Jerusalem"* (2 Chronicles 32:25). When Isaiah, the prophet, comes to him asking about the visitors from Babylon and King Hezekiah tells him all, not leaving out the fact that he had shown them all the treasure upon his property, Isaiah's response was to pronounce the Lord's judgement on Hezekiah's pride, *"Hear the word of the Lord: Behold, the days are coming, when all that is in your house, and that which your fathers have stored up till this day, shall be carried to Babylon. Nothing shall be left, says the Lord. And some of your own sons, who shall be born to you, shall be taken away...."* (2 Kings 20:16–18).

Even though we may repent of our sin, as in the case of Hezekiah, *"But Hezekiah humbled himself for the pride of his heart, both he and the inhabitants of Jerusalem, so that the wrath of the Lord did not come upon them in the days of Hezekiah"* (2 Chronicles 32:26), there are still consequences to pay and often times our families and others who are close to us are the ones who end up suffering as a result.

Lessons in Farm Life

Hezekiah's son was indeed taken captive to Babylon (2 Chronicles 33:11) and other descendants followed later on as well.

We find another familiar story of the pride and fall of a famous king in the fourth chapter of Daniel. Nebuchadnezzar, King of Babylon, who would have reigned a few generations after Hezekiah's time, was a very powerful king. We find in this account the revelation of another of Nebuchadnezzar's troubling dreams. After the failed attempts of his wise men to interpret this dream, he calls for Daniel, confident that he will have success where the others failed. *"… all the wise men of my kingdom are not able to make known to me the interpretation, but you are able, for the spirit of the holy gods is in you" (Daniel 4:18).* As God reveals the interpretation of the king's dream to Daniel, he is dismayed by it, for it reveals the humiliation that King Nebuchadnezzar will experience over an unknown period of time. In verse 27 Daniel encourages the king to change his ways, *"Therefore, O King, let my counsel be acceptable to you: break off your sins by practicing righteousness, and your iniquities by showing mercy to the oppressed, that there may perhaps be a lengthening of your prosperity."*

However, King Nebuchadnezzar neglects to follow Daniel's wise counsel and continues in his pride, *"At the end of twelve months he was walking on the roof of the royal palace of Babylon, and the king answered and said, Is not this great Babylon, which **I** have built by **my** mighty power as a royal residence and **for the glory of my majesty**?"* A voice came from heaven while the words were still in King

31

Pride Before a Call

Nebuchadnezzar's mouth, *"O King, to you it is spoken: The kingdom has departed from you, …" "Immediately the word was fulfilled against this proud king. Nebuchadnezzar was driven from among men and ate grass like an ox, and his body was wet with the dew of heaven till his hair grew as long as eagles' feathers, and his nails were like birds' claws, (Daniel 4:29-31, 33)"* This is not a very pretty picture, and certainly not a very dignified picture of a mighty king. King Nebuchadnezzar lived like an animal for 'seven periods of time', whether this may have been months or years, we are not told. All happened according to God's timing. This is a very good illustration of how God deals with a heart that is proud, *"Behold, I am against you, O proud one, declares the Lord God of Hosts, for your day has come, the time when I will punish you. The proud one shall stumble and fall, with none to raise him up"* (Jeremiah 50:31-32).

In God's timing and by God's grace, this once proud king does repent of his pride, and God restores his kingdom to him, *"At the end of my days I, Nebuchadnezzar, lifted my eyes to heaven, and my reason returned to me, and I blessed the Most High, and praised and honored him who lives forever, for his dominion is an everlasting dominion, and his kingdom endures from generation to generation, all the inhabitants of the earth are accounted as nothing, and he does according to his will among the host of heaven and among the inhabitants of the earth; and none can stay his hand or say to him, 'What have you done'"* (Daniel 4:34-35)?

This is a very clear example of God's mercy and grace to an undeserving sinner. King Nebuchadnezzar realized

Lessons in Farm Life

that God is indeed ruler of all, and one to be honored and praised; the King of heaven who is able to humble the proud, *"Now I, Nebuchadnezzar, praise and extol the King of heaven, for all his works are right and his ways are just; and those who walk in pride he is able to humble"* *(Daniel 4:37)*. We need to be careful that we not follow in Nebuchadnezzar's footsteps, stubbornly holding onto our pride, not seeking to please God in our actions, and ignoring the advice of those who are wiser and more mature in the faith than we are, *"… God opposes the proud but gives grace to the humble" (1 Peter 5:5)*.

We find a different set of circumstances involving the pride of another king in the book of 2 Chronicles chapter 26. Uzziah becomes king of Judah at the age of 16. He was a man who set himself to seek God, being instructed by Zechariah who had taught him the fear of God. As long as he sought the Lord, he prospered. Unfortunately, when he grew strong, he also grew proud, *"But when he was strong, he grew proud, to his destruction. For he was unfaithful to the Lord his God and entered the temple of the Lord to burn incense on the altar of incense," (2 Chronicles 26:16)*. Only the priests, the sons of Aaron were to burn incense, and the priests strongly rebuked Uzziah for his folly. Yet, instead of complying and leaving the temple, he became angry. The Lord then chastised Uzziah by striking him with leprosy. Even though we are not told whether or not Uzziah repented of his pride, we do know that he remained a leper to the day of his death.

Pride Before a Call

There are always consequences to pay for sin, even if repentance does occur. We find in the case of David's sin with Bathsheba, that even after David repented, he still had to pay the consequences, *"Nevertheless, because by this deed you have utterly scorned the Lord, the child who is born to you shall die" (2 Samuel 12:14)*. When the Lord afflicts David's child, David fasts and prays on its behalf, yet to no avail, for the child still dies. We need to constantly remind ourselves that there are always consequences as a result of sin, regardless of whether or not repentance occurs.

Jesus told the following parable for the benefit of some who thought themselves righteous and looked down their noses in contempt at other people. This is the familiar parable of the Pharisee and the tax collector where both men went up into the temple to pray. The Pharisee stood off by himself thanking God that he was not like other men, even the tax collector. Then he goes on to list off some of his righteous deeds, while the tax collector, *"... standing far off, would not even lift up his eyes to heaven, but beat his breast, saying, God, be merciful to me, a sinner! I tell you this man went down to his house justified, rather than the other. For everyone who exalts himself will be humbled, but the one who humbles himself will be exalted,"(Luke18:13-14)*. We need to pray to God that He keep us from this same self- righteous attitude of the Pharisee, being mindful that we are nothing apart from Christ. It is only by the grace of God, through the gift of faith that we have any righteousness at all. For God imputed Christ's righteousness to us, and our sin to Christ, *"For His sake I*

Lessons in Farm Life

have suffered the loss of all things and count them as rubbish, in order that I may gain Christ and be found in him, not having a righteousness of my own that comes from the law, but that which comes through faith in Christ, the righteousness from God that depends on faith" (Philippians 3:8-9).

These are just a few of many such cases in the Bible of people who displayed a proud heart and suffered the consequences because of it. I hope we can learn a valuable lesson from these examples. We need to be mindful not to think highly of ourselves because of our station in life. We need to be careful not to display pride and arrogance as did King Nebuchadnezzar, who was in a position of power and might, enjoying all the material blessings and honor that came with that position. God will not put up with a proud and haughty heart. He will humble us when we become arrogant in thinking ourselves to be better than those around us, just as he did King Nebuchadnezzar. We need to be mindful that if we have been blessed with a more prestigious position in life, enjoying all the benefits this position would entail, that it would only be due to the good Lord having put us there, and we should be humbly grateful for it. We should not look down on others if they happen not to be so blessed, and let us remember that true blessings are those that come from above, *"Blessed be the God and Father of our Lord Jesus Christ, who has blessed us in Christ with every spiritual blessing in the heavenly places, even as he chose us in him before the foundation of the world, that we should be holy and blameless before him" (Ephesians 1:3-4).*

Pride Before a Call

We also need to be careful that if we are not so fortunate as to be in as comfortable a position as our neighbor that we do not envy him. God may choose to have us in a more humble position physically in order to keep us in a more humble position spiritually, *"He has told you, O man, what is good; and what does the Lord require of you but to do justice, and to love kindness, and to walk humbly with your God?" (Micah 6:8). "He leads the humble in what is right, and teaches the humble His way. All the paths of the Lord are steadfast love and faithfulness, for those who keep his covenant and his testimonies" (Psalm 25:10).* We need also to remember not to think ourselves more righteous than others, as did the Pharisees. They led such rigid lifestyles, thinking that they could make themselves holy by following their many righteous rules and regulations. Although there are many do's and don't involved in a Christian's life- the outward display of 'following the rules' has nothing to do with whether one is a genuine Christian or not. A genuine Christian is one who (by God's grace) has been given the desire to obey his commands, due to the transforming work of the Holy Spirit.

We need also to be careful not to have a harsh and critical spirit toward a fellow believer who may be stumbling in his walk, falling into sin, and to remember that we are called to go along side that brother or sister in Christ, showing them such love and encouragement that he or she would be desirous to get back on the right path once again. Let us remember that- but for the grace of God, we ourselves could be in their shoes.

Lessons in Farm Life

We need to be showing compassion, not as the prophet, Jonah, who was so angry and displeased at God's mercy toward the people of Nineveh whom he thought to be undeserving of God's grace. This prophet of God, went outside the city to wait, in the hope that God would change his mind and destroy the city after all. God had graciously caused a plant to grow up in the night in order to save Jonah from the discomfort of sitting in the hot sun. Then, when God sends a worm to attack the plant so that it dies, we see Jonah's anger displayed once again as his response to the withering of the plant is; *"It is better for me to die than to live" (Jonah 4:8).*

May we follow in the example of Christ, displaying compassion for those who do not know Him, as he shows in his response to Jonah's anger, *"Do you do well to be angry for the plant? … You pity the plant, for which you did not labor, nor did you make it grow, which came into being in a night and perished in a night. And should not I pity Nineveh, that great city, in which there are more than 120,000 persons who do not know their right hand from their left, and also much cattle" (Jonah 4:9-11)?*

How many times do we also find ourselves showing more concern for the things of this world, than we do for those lost and dying within the world who are in need of a Savior? We need to live in a way that would show our understanding that people are far more important than things. The good Lord requires a right living from us- one that comes from a humble and obedient heart that is desirous to live in accordance to his word; *"He has told*

Pride Before a Call

you, O man, what is good, and what does the Lord require of you but to do justice, and to love kindness, and to walk humbly with your God?"(Micah 6:8). May we keep our hearts from pride and live with a desire to show a true humility of heart to all those we come in contact with.

4
Travelling On
Revelation 22:5

As I think back again to the many milk cows we have owned over the years, there is one I will remember not only with a certain amount of fondness, but with a fair bit of shame as well. This was the Jersey cow we had named Bambi at birth, because she had looked so much like a little fawn when she was born. She was a dark brown color and I must admit I had become rather attached to this beautiful bossy, so it was with a great sense of sadness that I reconciled myself to selling her. We were at the Lakeville farm at the time and were getting ready to sell and move to a larger property. As this other property needed much work, we decided it would be best to sell off the animals we had and wait to get more until we were properly equipped to care for them.

Travelling On

I was comforted in knowing that Bambi was going to a good home as we were familiar with the family that decided to take her. We had also made arrangements to be able to keep the calf she would have after it was weaned. However, this did not lessen the remorse that I felt the morning I knew she would be leaving us. I recall going out to the barn with a large horse brush. Is there even such a thing as a cow brush? How many people brush their cows down anyway? Well, I went out and started brushing Bambi's soft brown coat and as I did so, the tears started coming. Even now as I think of it, my eyes are pricking suspiciously. How foolish I feel even thinking of that day. For when the fellow showed up with his trailer to load Bambi onto, I felt the tears start coming again. I couldn't help myself, they just flowed. I apologized, feeling ridiculous for my being such a sentimental sap over a silly cow. As it turned out Bambi wasn't any more eager to leave than I was to have her leave. She gave us all quite a battle about getting on that trailer. I was so thankful that this man showed such patience and long suffering in his dealing with my stubborn bossy and also with my foolish display of sentimentality. It was distressing to have this ordeal take so much longer than it should have. However, after much patient prodding and a little ingenuity on the part of Bambi's new owner, we finally did get her onto the trailer and she was off to her new home with her former owner weeping to see her go.

Thinking back on this memory of some years ago made me realize how attached we can become to the

40

Lessons in Farm Life

things of this earth. The Bible tells us to set our minds on things above, not on earthly pleasures, *"Set your minds on things that are above, not on things that are on earth" (Colossians 3:2). "Do not lay up for yourselves treasures on earth, where moth and rust destroy and where thieves break in and steal, but lay up for yourselves treasures in heaven, where neither moth nor rust destroys and where thieves do not break in and steal. For where your treasure is, there your heart will be also" (Matthew 6:19-21).* As Christians, our concerns should not be on earthly pleasures, accumulation of wealth and worldly possessions. Our concern should be with doing the will of God, *"Do not love the world or the things in the world. If anyone loves the world, the love of the Father is not in him. For all that is in the world-the desires of the flesh and the desires of the eyes and pride in possessions-is not from the Father but is from the world. And the world is passing away along with its desires, but whoever does the will of God abides forever" (1 John 2:15-17).* We brought nothing with us into this world and the Bible assures us that we will not take anything out of it when we leave. The material possessions that we accumulate are things that we will enjoy on this earth for a very brief space of time. We do not even know how long. The good Lord may choose to have us live a long and full life on this earth or we may not be granted many years here at all. We just don't know. So we really need to be making the best use of whatever amount of time God has chosen to give us.

We need to have our focus in the right place, remembering that the goal of all Christians should be to

41

Travelling On

glorify God in everything that we do, living in this world to honor Him, and being careful not to blend in with the rest of the world. The Bible is very clear in teaching that friendship with the world makes us an enemy with God, *"You adulterous people! Do you not know that friendship with the world is enmity with God? Therefore whoever wishes to be a friend of the world makes himself an enemy of God"* *(James 4:4).* This of course does not mean that we are to be unfriendly towards those who do not embrace our faith. It does, however, mean we are not to embrace the ways of the world. Naturally we should not ostracize ourselves from unbelievers, for how could we be an effective witness to them if we refuse to have any contact with them? Unfortunately, so many who call themselves Christians have their own little circle, a 'holy huddle' we may call it, those they choose to spend most of their time with, and in doing so neglect to spend any time trying to reach out to those most in need of it. By ones 'in need' I refer to those unbelievers they may even rub shoulders with on a day to day basis, whether at school or at work; also those who may be new in the faith and in need of encouragement through more Christian contact.

I remember a time, years ago now, that I (most ashamedly) must admit to feeling a slight resentment to newcomers in our church. We were quite small at that time and of course everyone knew everyone else. I was a rather introverted person (I always despised being referred to in that way, but must admit it to be true). It was hard for me to get to know people, probably because I was so self

Lessons in Farm Life

conscious and afraid of saying the wrong thing. Anyway, I look back at that time of several years ago now and shake my head. What a terrible way for a 'Christian' to be. I was so self- absorbed, not at all concerned for the needs of others in the way I should have been. I thank God for the work he has done to change that in my life. I'm afraid too many of us who call ourselves Christians are lovers of ourselves more than we are lovers of God. This is the way the world encourages us to be.

As ones who profess Christ, we are to show ourselves to be different from the world, *"But you are a chosen race, a royal priesthood, a holy nation, a people for his own possession, that you may proclaim the excellencies of him who called you out of darkness into his marvelous light" (1 Peter 2:9).* Our Lord has called us out of the darkness of sin and led us into the light of His presence,*"Therefore be imitators of God, as beloved children. And walk in love, as Christ loved us and gave Himself up for us, a fragrant offering and sacrifice to God" (Ephesians 5:1).*

Do we really try to comprehend exactly what it means to be a child of God? God is actually our *Father*, we are his children and he loves us as he loves His only begotten Son, Jesus Christ. As our Father, we are to talk to him in prayer. This is the model that we are to use when we pray to our Heavenly Father; *"Our Father in heaven, hallowed be your name. Your kingdom come, your will be done, on earth as it is in heaven. Give us this day our daily bread, and forgive us our debts, as we forgive our debtors. And lead us not into temptation, but deliver us from evil" (Matthew 6:9-13).* I

Travelling On

remember someone once saying, an easy way to remember the way we should pray is to think of the word ACTS; A is for adoration, we are to praise our God; C is for confession, we need to confess our sins before him. T is for thanksgiving, we have many things with which to thank our Heavenly Father. S is for supplication; lastly we come before our God to ask our petitions of him. We should be mindful that the prayer requests we take before our Father should be with the understanding that His will must be done, not ours. We should not selfishly ask for things to satisfy our own desires, remembering that we are to be laying up treasure in heaven and not on this earth.

We are not to merge ourselves with the world in such a way that others would not be able to tell us apart from non Christians,*"Do not be conformed to this world, but be transformed by the renewal of your mind…" (Romans 12:2).* In Deuteronomy 26:18-19 we find these verses, *"And the Lord has declared today that you are a people for his treasured possession, as he has promised you, and that you are to keep all His commandments, and that He will set you in praise and in fame and in honor high above all nations that he has made, and that you shall be a people holy to the Lord your God, as he promised."* In the King James version we find this translation of verse 18, *"And the Lord hath avouched thee this day to be his peculiar people…"* meaning distinctive. We are to be set apart, different, not like the rest of the world.

One of the ways we should show this difference is in the way we respond to a confrontation, or in times of stress and trial. We should be able to respond to difficult

Lessons in Farm Life

situations in a way that would be uncharacteristic of the world, *"Do all things without grumbling or questioning, that you may be blameless and innocent, children of God without blemish in the midst of a crooked and twisted generation, among whom you shine as lights in the world, holding fast to the word of life,..." (Philippians 2:14-16).* We are to shine as lights in a dark world being alert and watchful, looking forward to the coming of our Lord, *"But you are not in darkness, brothers, for that day to surprise you like a thief. For you are all children of light, children of the day. We are not of the night or of the darkness. So then let us not sleep, as others do, but let us keep awake and be sober" (1 Thessalonians 5:4-6).*

We should live as faithful examples of followers of Christ, remembering that the witness and testimony of our lives may be the only gospel some people are ever exposed to. I remember hearing this little saying in a sermon I listened to some time ago: 'We are writing a gospel, a chapter each day, by the deeds that we do and the words that we say, men read what you write, distorted or true, so what is the gospel according to you?' We need to be mindful that others are watching us. Let us be wary of doing or saying anything that could give unbelievers an excuse not to have any desire to embrace our faith. May we, each and every one, be impressed with the tremendous responsibility that is ours to live faithful, consistent, Christian lives, setting the kind of example that would prompt others to ask us of the hope that we have within us.

45

Travelling On

We are to live in the world and yet not of the world, remembering that this is not our home, *"They are not of the world, just as I am not of the world" (John 17:16).* We are just journeying on, passing through onto a much better destination. Our time on this earth is brief, *"Man is like a breath: his days are like a passing shadow" (Psalm 144:4).* Yet when we arrive at our final destination which is heaven, we will be there for all of eternity, *"And night will be no more. They will need no light of lamp or sun, for the Lord God will be their light and they will reign forever and ever,"* (Revelation 22:5).

We are citizens of heaven and should live giving every indication of that citizenship, *"So then you are no longer strangers and aliens, but you are fellow citizens with the saints and members of the household of God,"* (Ephesians *2:19-21). "But our citizenship is in heaven, and from it we await a Savior, the Lord Jesus Christ, who will transform our lowly body to be like His glorious body, by the power that enables Him even to subject all things to Himself" (Philippians 3:20).* What a glorious expectation for all those who are in the faith. These lowly decaying bodies of ours will be transformed instantly into incorruptible bodies that will never grow old. Just think of it, no more aching bones, no sickness or disease, just perfect bodies that will never wear out. In 1 Corinthians 15:52-57 we find, *"...in a moment, in the twinkling of an eye, at the last trumpet. For the trumpet will sound and the dead will be raised imperishable, and we shall be changed. For this perishable body must put on imperishable, and this mortal body must put on immortality.*

Lessons in Farm Life

When the perishable puts on the imperishable, and the mortal puts on immortality, then shall come to pass the saying that is written: Death is swallowed up in victory. O death, where is your victory? O death, where is your sting? The sting of death is sin, and the power of sin is the law. But thanks be to God, who gives us the victory through our Lord Jesus Christ."

When our time on this earth is through we can look forward to a much better life with our Heavenly Father, where we are promised there will be no more pain, no trials, no suffering, just an eternity giving honor and glory to the One who has made it possible for us to be there, *"For I consider that the sufferings of this present time are not worth comparing with the glory that is to be revealed to us" (Romans 8:18).* In Revelation 7:15-17 we read, *"Therefore they are before the throne of God, and serve Him day and night in His temple; and he who sits on the throne will shelter them with His presence. They shall hunger no more, neither thirst anymore; the sun shall not strike them, nor any scorching heat. For the Lamb in the midst of the throne will be their shepherd, and He will guide them to springs of living water, and God will wipe away every tear from their eyes."* Oh what a day that will be.

May we, as Christians, be living faithful consistent lives in this world, alert and watchful, expectant even of the coming of our Lord and Savior. May we be careful to be storing up our treasures in heaven and not to become overly attached to the things of this earth. Let us be mindful that we are being prepared for a much better and

Travelling On

more glorious life one day as we look forward to 'travelling on' to our future home in heaven.

5

Out of Sight Out of Mind

1 Corinthians 10:24

Shortly after I started writing these stories, my daughter reminded me of another amusing tale from the Lakeville farm. We had been raising wild turkeys at this time and if you've ever seen a wild turkey you will know they, especially the toms, are a fair size larger than the white domestic turkeys. In fact a friend driving by one day noticed our tom following behind one of our young children. The bird was almost as big as the child, and he was quite aghast, fearing for our child's safety. We reassured him the children were quite safe. We had raised these birds from hatchlings and they were as tame as the domestic ones. These birds loved to follow along behind my husband as well, especially when he would take the

Out of Sight Out of Mind

tiller out to the garden. It was not unusual to see them following closely behind the tiller snatching up some delectable treats as they pecked their way along. They were actually picking out the worms from my garden, which I was not terribly thrilled about.

Anyway, one day we noticed that one of our turkeys was missing. We had no idea where she had gone to and concluding that something must have made a nice meal of her, we dismissed our missing bird from our minds. It was probably a few weeks later when my husband received a phone call from one of the neighbors. Apparently his wife had told him she had been hearing strange noises out in the woods behind their house. Then earlier that day he had gotten his tiller out to till up some ground. He took a trip or two down the rows, then sensing that he was not alone turned to find this huge brown bird directly behind him. It likely took quite a hike out of him at the time. Of course, our bird meant him no harm, she was just looking for some tasty morsels and she knew she could find some at the sound of the tiller. After our neighbor's initial shock, he gave my husband a call to ask whether we were missing any livestock. So, we happily retrieved our missing bird taking care to have her better supervised in future.

Thinking back on this episode of our hobby farming exploits made me think of the importance of keeping others in mind. We should never dismiss someone from our mind just because we no longer see them on a regular basis. I'm thinking of families that may have been a part

Lessons in Farm Life

of our worship services and yet are no longer with us. Perhaps they have moved away, or maybe they are not attending our local church for another reason that we may not even be aware of. We should keep them in our prayers and let them know we still care for them by keeping in touch, and tell them that we would happily welcome them back, if it were possible for them to consider returning to our local fellowship.

I'm also thinking of different ones within our local church that may need encouragement. The Bible is very clear in this area. We must be encouraging one another, *"Therefore encourage one another and build one another up," (1 Thessalonians 5:11).* Often times we are informed of different ones within the congregation who may be ailing physically or discouraged spiritually. There may be some who are new in the faith and could use encouragement in spiritual matters. How many times do we think to ourselves; 'Yes, we should visit that person or those people this week, or even just give them a call if we are unable to visit,' and then go back to our homes and completely put them out of our mind? I'm afraid this probably happens a fair bit of the time. We need to make a more conscientious effort to encourage those who are in need of it, showing our love through our service to others, being desirous to hear these words from our Master one day; *"Well, done good and faithful servant..." (Matthew 25:21).*

Why is it we should be ready and willing to serve those around us? Is it to gain acceptance with God? It may be so that we can feel better about ourselves, or perhaps so

Out of Sight Out of Mind

others will think more highly of us, or could it be to make ourselves appear to be a little more righteous? Of course it should not be for any of those reasons; for the Bible tells us that even our best deeds are as filthy rags, *"...and all our righteous deeds are like a polluted garment" (Isaiah 64:6).*

When James says; *"Confess your faults one to another, and pray one for another, that you may be healed. The effectual fervent prayer of a righteous man availeth much" (James 5:16),* he isn't talking about the righteousness that we, ourselves possess. I remember remarking to my husband one day on this verse; I told him I really don't know how effective my prayers can be, because I just don't feel very righteous. He told me something that greatly relieved my mind and gave me renewed confidence that God would hear my prayers. He said that we need to remember that when God looks on us, it is Christ's righteousness that He sees, not ours. For the only righteousness that we have is that of Christ's, which is imputed to us. Therefore, we can go to our Heavenly Father in complete confidence knowing that He will hear and answer our prayers, according to His will.

If we cannot do good in order to gain acceptance with God, or so others will think more highly of us, or so we can feel better about ourselves, why would we even try to do good? The main reason for us to do good for others is out of love for our great God and Savior, Jesus Christ, who has redeemed us from our sins, *"Everyone who believes that Jesus is the Christ has been born of God, and everyone who loves the Father loves whoever has been born*

52

Lessons in Farm Life

of Him. By this we know that we love the children of God, when we love God and obey His commandments" (1 John 5:1-2). We should be doing good in order to show our love and to glorify our God. In a biography of Thomas Jackson, the famous general of the Civil War, we find this statement; "He never missed an opportunity to credit his Heavenly Father with any success he might have had on the battlefield." Reverend Ewing said of him, "He did not pray to men, but to God... He seemed to feel more than any man I ever knew the danger of robbing God of the glory due for our success." We too, should be careful to give all the glory to God in any successes that we ourselves experience, regardless of how big or how small they may be, *"As each has received a gift, use it to serve one another, as good stewards of God's varied grace: whoever speaks, as one who speaks oracles of God; whoever serves, as one who serves by the strength that God supplies–in order that in everything God may be glorified through Jesus Christ"* (1 Peter 4:10-11).

In *Matthew 25:34-40*, we read of the important significance of doing good for others,"... *'Come, you who are blessed by my Father, inherit the kingdom prepared for you from the foundation of the world. For I was hungry and you gave me food, I was thirsty and you gave me drink, I was a stranger and you welcomed me, I was naked and you clothed me, I was sick and you visited me, I was in prison and you came to me.'" Then the righteous will answer him, saying, Lord, when did we see you hungry and feed you, or thirsty and give you drink? And when did we see you a stranger and welcome you, or naked and clothe you? And when did we see*

Out of Sight Out of Mind

you sick or in prison and visit you? And the King will answer them, 'Truly, I say to you, as you did it to one of the least of these my brothers, you did it to me'." We need to remember that in doing good deeds for others, it as if we are doing them for our Lord. This should be a great motivation for us. As a result of our love for our God, we should be filled with a desire to be obedient to His will. In His word He tells us, *"And let us not grow weary of doing good, for in due season we will reap, if we do not give up. So, then, as we have opportunity, let us do good to everyone, and especially to those who are of the household of faith" (Galatians 6:9-10).*

Another very good reason for availing ourselves in service to others is that we follow Christ's example when we do so. In the gospel of John we find the story of how Jesus washed the disciples' feet, *"When He had washed their feet and put on His outer garments and resumed his place, He said to them, 'Do you understand what I have done to you? You call me Teacher and Lord, and you are right, for so I am. If I then, your Lord and Teacher have washed your feet, you also ought to wash one another's feet. For I have given you an example, that you also should do just as I have done to you"* *(John 13:12-15).* Now this does not mean that we should literally wash one another's feet, unless there would be an appropriate circumstance for doing so. However, given the fact that the men of Jesus' time would have done a tremendous amount of walking in open sandals, therefore making their feet dirty and dusty, this was an appropriate act of service that Jesus did for His disciples. The point is that we need to be willing to humble ourselves as Jesus did

Lessons in Farm Life

and be more than willing to serve rather than be served. Our Lord humbled Himself even to the point of death upon the cross.

If we could just comprehend exactly what that meant, for Christ to experience the full wrath of God, His Heavenly Father, in taking upon himself the penalty for all of the sins of His people; past, present, and future. They are all forgiven in Christ. We can't even begin to contemplate what a horrendous experience that must have been for our Lord. He humbled Himself through his incarnation, coming to this earth to be born as a baby and suffering all the miseries of this life. Our Lord experienced the curse of death upon the cross on our behalf- and even remained under the power of death for a time.

The Bible tells us he was a man of sorrows, *"He was despised and rejected by men; a man of sorrows, and acquainted with grief; and as one from whom men hide their faces. He was despised, and we esteemed Him not. Surely He has borne our griefs and carried our sorrows; yet we esteemed Him stricken, smitten by God and afflicted. But He was wounded for our transgressions; He was crushed for our iniquities; upon Him was the chastisement that brought us peace, and with His stripes we are healed" (Isaiah 53:3-5).*

He suffered greatly knowing what He was about to face. He *"...knelt down and prayed, saying, Father, if you are willing remove this cup from me. Nevertheless, not my will, but yours, be done...And being in agony He prayed more earnestly; His sweat became like great drops of blood falling down to the ground" (Luke 22:41-42, 44).* Indeed our Lord

Out of Sight Out of Mind

knew just what He was about to suffer. He was to suffer the wrath of God in our place, *"Since, therefore, we have been justified by his blood, much more shall we be saved by him from the wrath of God" (Romans 5:9).* He experienced death and hell, along with the agony of the abandonment of His Father, *"And at the ninth hour Jesus cried with a loud voice, 'Eloi, Eloi, lema sabachthani?'" which means, "My God, My God, why have you forsaken me" (Matthew 27:46)?*

Do we ever stop and think of what an eternity experiencing the wrath of God, while being separated from the love of God would be like? In Luke 16 verses 19 to 30 we find the parable of the rich man and Lazarus. We are given an inkling of what hell will be like as the rich man speaks of being in torment and anguish. In Revelation 20 we find John's account of his vision, *"And I saw the dead, great and small, standing before the throne, and books were opened. Then another book was opened, which is the book of life. And the dead were judged by what was written in the books, according to what they had done. And the sea gave up the dead who were in it, Death and Hades gave up the dead who were in them, and they were judged, each one of them, according to what they had done. Then Death and Hades were thrown into the lake of fire. This is the second death, the lake of fire. And if anyone's name was not found written in the book of life, he was thrown into the lake of fire" (Revelation 20: 12-15).* If our names are written in the book of life then we have been saved from this second death, thanks to our great God and Savior, Jesus

56

Lessons in Farm Life

Christ. He went to that cross in our place. We deserved to be there, He didn't.

How can we ever even begin to repay such a vast debt of love? The answer is simple. Of course, we cannot. However, we can strive to live wholeheartedly in service for our Lord, doing good for others, *"Let no one seek his own good, but the good of his neighbor" (1 Corinthians 10:24)*. We need to deny ourselves, saying 'no' to our selfish ambitions and 'yes' to service for our Lord. We do this by keeping others in mind and availing ourselves in service to others for the sake of our Lord out of love for all that He has accomplished on our behalf.

6

Stubborn and Stiff-necked

Exodus 32:9

As a family we have gathered to celebrate many Thanksgivings over the years, but there is one that is most indelibly imprinted upon my mind. It was our fourth year at the Weston farm and I had invited my whole family to our place to share the Thanksgiving meal together. We had a young heifer for sale at the time and, as it turned out, a man from Grand Falls came to look at her that very day. I thought he could have picked a better time than the Thanksgiving Holiday. However, it was certainly providential that he did pick this particular day, when we happened to have several men on hand, for as it turned out, we needed to call on the services of each and every one of them.

58

Lessons in Farm Life

This fellow had a pony with him that he was trying to sell, and our daughter, who was an avid horse lover at that time, took quite a fancy to this pony. The pony seemed to be well trained and we thought it would make a nice starter horse for her. Since our oldest son took on the bulk of the responsibility for the cows during this period, he suggested we should trade his Jersey steer for this black and white pony. It was a very generous offer on the part of our son. However, his husky steer was in no way, shape, or form, going to agree to have any part in this arrangement. He was *not* going to be traded for that pony if he had any say in the matter.

I was pleased that this fellow decided he would take our little heifer, Cindy, though even she gave the fellows a bit of a hard time getting her on the back of the truck. However, in comparison to the show our son's steer put on, she was actually quite cooperative. Our son's Jersey steer had absolutely no intentions whatsoever of setting one hoof on the back of that truck. The scene that followed would surely have won the funniest home video award, if there even was such a thing anymore. Absolutely no amount of pushing, pulling, coaxing or bribing would convince this fellow to budge an inch. He lay down on the ground with his stubborn nose in the air and his legs sprawled out at his side and refused to budge. My father finally came up with the idea of using a strap to slide under his belly so as to pull him onto the back of the truck. So this was the strategy they employed. After maneuvering the strap under the steer, one of the men then linked it

59

Stubborn and Stiff-necked

to the inside of the truck box. This was when the real fun began. With at least 6 men on one end pulling on the strap we literally had a tug of war on our hands; one rebel of a steer against six good-sized men. It really was a hilarious sight to behold. Thankfully, the men eventually won out. After exerting themselves with their tugging and pulling they finally did get that cantankerous beast moved up onto the back of the truck, but he sure didn't make it one bit easy for them. That was one stubborn steer.

We may get exasperated with the stubbornness of such animals, however, we must realize that we can be just as stubborn as people. We can find many references to the stubbornness of the Israelites in the Bible. One such instance is found in Exodus when Moses receives the Ten Commandments from God on Mount Sinai. God tells Moses to go back down to his people for they had corrupted themselves by the making of a golden calf. When Moses had not returned as quickly as the people felt he should have, they convinced Aaron to make a golden calf so they could worship it. By worshipping this idol they had turned their backs on God, *"And the Lord said to Moses, I have seen this people, and behold, it is a stiff-necked people"(Exodus 32:9).* Not surprisingly, people are the same today as they were back in the time of the Israelites. We can be just as stubborn and stiff-necked, soon forgetting our God and following in our own stubborn ways, worshipping our own kinds of idols.

In Judges Chapter 2, we find another example of Israel's stubbornness and rebellion. Due to Israel's failure

Lessons in Farm Life

to complete the conquest God had commanded them, they were to suffer the consequences; *"...you have not obeyed my voice. What is this you have done? So now I say, I will not drive them out before you, but they shall become thorns in your sides, and their gods shall be a snare to you."* Indeed, this is what happened as we read down in verse 13, *"They abandoned the Lord and served the Baals and the Ashtaroth.* And as a result, *".. He sold them into the hand of their surrounding enemies, so that they could no longer withstand their enemies."*

We may shake our heads at the foolishness of the Israelites knowing full well of the warnings they had been given, **"Be very careful, therefore, to love the Lord your God. For if you turn back and cling to the remnant of these nations** *remaining among you and make marriages with them, so that you associate with them and they with you, know for certain that the Lord your God will no longer drive out these nations before you, but* **they shall be a snare and a trap for you, a whip on your sides and thorns in your eyes,** *until you perish from off this good ground that the Lord your God has given you" (Joshua 23:11–13).*

God's people fail to listen to His instructions today as well, disregarding his clear admonishments. God very clearly told the people that in obedience they could expect blessing and in disobedience they could expect consequences, *"See, I am setting before you today a blessing and a curse: the blessing, if you obey the commandments of the Lord your God, ...and the curse, if you do not obey the*

Stubborn and Stiff-necked

commandments of the Lord your God, but turn aside from the way that I am commanding you" (Deuteronomy 11:26-28).

Why do we tempt our God as the Israelites did? The warnings given in the Old Testament still apply to us today. One of those commands was not to intermarry with the pagan nations, meaning we should not marry outside of our faith. A professing believer should not even consider dating or courting someone who does not share their same faith. If we do this, we are putting ourselves in the path of temptation. Many times this may lead to marriage and then the consequences to our disobedience will follow as a result.

In the ninth chapter of Nehemiah we find another of many reminders of how the people continued to forsake the Lord, *"Nevertheless, **they were disobedient and rebelled against you** and cast your law behind their back and killed your prophets, who had warned them in order to turn them back to you, and they committed great blasphemies. **Therefore you gave them into the hand of their enemies, who made them suffer.** And in the time of their suffering they cried out to you and you heard them from heaven and according to your great mercies you gave them saviors who saved them from the hand of their enemies. But after they had rest they did evil again before you, and you abandoned them to the hand of their enemies, so that they had dominion over them. **Yet when they turned and cried to you, you heard from heaven, and many times you delivered them according to your mercies.** And you warned them in order to turn them back to your law. **Yet they acted presumptuously and did not obey your***

62

Lessons in Farm Life

commandments, but sinned against your rules, which if a person does them, he shall live by them, and turned a stubborn shoulder and stiffened their neck and would not obey. *Many years you bore with them and warned them by your Spirit through your prophets. Yet they would not give ear. Therefore you gave them into the hand of the peoples of the lands.* **Nevertheless, in your great mercies you did not make an end of them or forsake them, for you are a gracious and merciful God"** *(Nehemiah 9:26-31).*

How undeserving we are of God's great mercy and long suffering toward us. What a comfort to know that He truly is a gracious and merciful God. We can go to Him in any and all circumstances, regardless of how great a mess we have made of our lives, knowing that when we are repentant, He will forgive us. We find a very fitting illustration of this in Luke chapter 15 in the story of the prodigal son. This father was not just waiting for his wayward son to return, he was waiting and watching; and when he spied him, he ran to him with joy, *"But while he was still a long way off, his father saw him and felt compassion, and ran and embraced him and kissed him."* There was no condemnation, no wagging of the finger or reproachful speech. This father was overjoyed to have his son back once again. It is the same with our Lord and heavenly Father. He also rejoices over the return of his wayward sons and daughters when they display before him a heart of repentance. In those times we are reminded of the great mercy of our Lord, and how imperative it is that we continually draw near to Him.

63

Stubborn and Stiff-necked

We truly must realize how we, as Christians, are totally dependent on God for everything and in all circumstances. The Bible tells us that we are to draw near to God, *"Submit yourselves to God. Resist the devil, and he will flee from you. Draw near to God, and He will draw near to you" (James 4:7–8).* If we really love God as we should, we *will* draw near to Him- by reading and studying our Bibles, spending time in prayer and availing ourselves to the means of his word as much as possible. We will also strive to overcome the devil's temptations, desiring to resist his many tactics to lure us into giving in to our sinful desires.

It seems as if professing Christians are, more times than not, prone to draw near to God when we are in trouble or facing various trials. That is when we feel totally helpless and cry out to God to 'bail us out'. Does this not sound familiar? We need to be reminded of this particular verse in 2 Chronicles; *"The Lord is with you, while you are with him; and if you seek him, he will be found of you; but if you forsake him, he will forsake you" (2 Chronicles 15:2).* We must realize that if we totally forsake him, (never to return,) we did not belong to him to begin with. The Bible clearly teaches that God will not forsake those who are His, *"...for he has said, I will never leave you nor forsake you (Hebrews 13:5).* He will, however, allow his children to follow their own desires for a time- in order to teach us to be totally dependent on Him. In this way, we are reminded of the importance of drawing near to God *every* day, not just in times of trouble as the nation of Israelite

64

Lessons in Farm Life

did when they were oppressed by their enemies. We must understand that we will suffer the consequences to our disobedience if we fail to adhere to God's instructions as well. We need to be careful not to follow in the Israelites' footsteps, calling out to God, and drawing near to Him in earnest, only in times of difficulty, and then, when everything is going fairly smoothly return to relying on ourselves again, fooling ourselves into thinking that we can handle everything on our own. Living a faithful consistent, Christian life is a daily battle. We need God's help each and every day to fight the battle over sin and live victoriously.

When we find ourselves going through many trials or much suffering, do we wonder why this is? Have we ever asked ourselves if we are being punished by God? We must understand, God does not punish his people for their wrong behavior. Christ paid the punishment for our sins, (Hebrews 10:14). God is a just God. He will not make us pay for something that has already been covered. One of the reasons we may experience trials and suffering, could be for the strengthening of our faith in order to lead us to a deeper obedience, *"Count it all joy, my brothers, when you meet trials of various kinds, for you know that the testing of your faith produces steadfastness" (James 1:2-3)* which will display God's works and bring Him glory, (John 9:1-3).

We know there is a reason for everything that happens. There was a reason why God gave the Israelites into the hands of their enemies. It was due to judgment on the

Stubborn and Stiff-necked

nation for their rebellion against God. They suffered the consequences to their disobedience as God had clearly told them they would do. If they had paid careful attention to God's instructions, and obeyed Him, they wouldn't have had to suffer the consequence of disobedience, (Deuteronomy 11:26-28). We can learn a valuable lesson from the Israelites' failure to obey God's commands.

While it is true God uses our trials to strengthen our faith, it is also true that another reason for suffering *may* be as a result of our disobedience to God's instructions. As a part of God's family, we are under his care, and if we fail to receive God's discipline, which is his instruction through His word for training in righteousness, we can expect to suffer the consequences to our disobedience, *"have you forgotten the exhortation that addresses you as sons? 'My son, do not regard lightly the discipline of the Lord, nor be weary when reproved by him. For the Lord disciplines the one he loves, and chastises every son whom he receives.'* **It is for discipline that you have to endure**. *God is treating you as sons. For what son is there whom his father does not discipline"* (*Hebrews 12:5-7*)? Discipline is given for the purpose of correction, to mold and make us more into the image of Christ. God disciplines us through his word to correct our behavior and to bring us back into a right relationship with Him, *"As many as I love, I reprove and discipline: be zealous therefore and repent"* (*Revelation 3:19*).

How often do we find ourselves stubbornly holding on to our old ways of doing things even when we know those old ways are opposed to God's instructions?

66

Lessons in Farm Life

God's word clearly admonishes us to put away our old practices, *"Put to death therefore what is earthly in you: sexual immorality, impurity, passion, evil desire, and covetousness, which is idolatry. On account of these the wrath of God is coming. In these you too once walked, when you were living in them. But now you must put them all away: anger, wrath, malice, slander, and obscene talk from your mouth. Do not lie to one another, seeing that you have put off the old self with its practices and put on the new self, which is being renewed in knowledge after the image of its creator" (Colossians 3:5-10).*

When we fail to obey God's teaching, we must expect to suffer the consequences of that disobedience. We can be so like the Israelites, who followed a vicious cycle, living faithfully for a while, then straying off the path to serve other gods; and when having experienced the consequences of their disobedience, seeking God's help and deliverance. Then after all goes well for a time, the whole cycle starts all over again. Unfortunately, many of us who profess to know Christ do not live any more faithfully than they did back then, as we also can be a very stubborn and stiff-necked people. So often we are bent on having our own way and doing our own thing regardless of what we know God requires of us. We need also to be careful that we are not stubbornly serving the gods of this world. According to the dictionary, one of the definitions of a god is a person or thing of supreme value. We may not be bowing down to an actual man-made statue, but we may be putting other people or things on a higher plane than the One true God of heaven and earth, *"You shall*

Stubborn and Stiff-necked

worship the Lord your God, and Him only shall you serve" *(Luke 4:8).* When we fail to worship God in the way he has outlined for us in his word as we should, we can expect to suffer the consequences of our disobedience.

We must realize that God does not treat his people any differently today than He did back then, in the time of the Israelites. When we live in obedience to God's word, we can expect to be blessed and when we live in disobedience, we can expect to suffer the consequences of that disobedience. When I speak of being blessed, I'm not talking about being prosperous materially, for that is clearly not scriptural. When we think of being blessed by God, what should come to our minds? In Numbers 6:22-27 we find the Lord speaking to Moses, saying, *"Speak to Aaron and his sons, saying, Thus you shall bless the people of Israel: you shall say to them, **The Lord bless you and keep you; the Lord make his face to shine upon you and be gracious to you; the Lord lift up his countenance upon you and give you peace.** So shall they put my name upon the people of Israel, and I will bless them."* To have the Lord shine his face upon us, to experience His grace and peace within our lives- that is what it means to be truly blessed by God.

We are not promised a road of comfort and ease, quite the contrary, rather. The Christian life is one that may be filled with many trials, *"I have said these things to you, that in me you may have peace. In the world you will have tribulation. But take heart; I have overcome the world"* *(John 16:33).* Thankfully, we can know that in Christ, we also can overcome tribulation. We can even

Lessons in Farm Life

experience joy in trials knowing they are brought into our lives for a purpose- in order to develop perseverance and that in turn will produce maturity in our faith. Any time we experience trials, suffering or tribulation of any kind we should remember it is all for our sanctification. Christ suffered before us and for us and we should not be surprised when we suffer as well, (Hebrews 2:10-11).

What a relief and comfort it is to know that when we suffer due to our disobedience, God will indeed forgive our sins when we turn *from* our wicked ways and turn *to* our God. In 2 Chronicles 7:14 we read, *"...if my people who are called by my name will humble themselves, and pray and seek my face and turn from their wicked ways, then I will hear from heaven and will forgive their sin..."* We have to realize, however, that in coming to our God, it must be in a state of repentance, with a hatred of that sin and a desire to utterly forsake it.

If only we, as Christians today, would have a heart of repentance as Ezra did in finding out that the people had invited God's wrath upon them due to their intermarrying with the pagan nations, *"As soon as I heard this, I tore my garment and my cloak and pulled hair from my head and beard and sat appalled ... until the evening sacrifice. And at the evening sacrifice I rose from my fasting, with my garment and my cloak torn, and fell upon my knees and spread out my hands to the Lord my God, saying: 'O my God, I am ashamed and blush to lift my face to you, my God, for our iniquities have risen higher than our heads, and our guilt has mounted up to the heavens" (Ezra 9:3-6).* While Ezra himself had

Stubborn and Stiff-necked

not committed this trespass, he was nevertheless in a great state of distress because of the sins of the people, as we can see in his prayer throughout most of the ninth chapter of Ezra. Thankfully the people themselves came to realize the severity of their sin as they confess it before God in the following chapter. What a wonderfully patient and long-suffering God we serve. What a tremendous blessing it is to know that He will forgive our trespasses if we confess our sins to Him, *"If we confess our sins, He is faithful and just to forgive us our sins and to cleanse us from all unrighteousness" (1 John 1:9).*

However, we still need to be careful not to use the knowledge of God's grace in such a way that we become careless towards sin. We do not want to take the view that if we sin, it's no big deal, for God will forgive us. We find Paul speaking here in Romans 6:1-2, *"What shall we say then? Are we to continue in sin that grace may abound? By no means! How can we who died to sin still live in it?"* Paul's point here is that a believer's condition has changed so drastically by his union with Christ that not only would it be inappropriate for him to keep on sinning as he had before, it would actually be impossible for him/her to do so. Now, of course this does not mean that we will not sin, for we certainly will not reach a sinless state on this earth- because we live with a sin nature. Our natural bent is to sin. However, if we are walking in step with the Spirit, 'sin no longer reigns in our lives', it remains, but it does not reign any longer. It doesn't control us as it once did. As ones who have been converted to Christ,

Lessons in Farm Life

we have the benefit of God's Holy Spirit within our lives, and as we seek him, he teaches us in the way we should go, *"But the Helper, the Holy Spirit, whom the Father will send in my name, he will teach you all things and bring to your remembrance all that I have said to you" (John 14:26).* As those who are in Him, Christ has set us free from the bondage of sin, so we truly can be victorious over it. Therefore, if stubbornness and rebellion are areas within our lives that we struggle with, we can conquer them by God's grace with the help of His Holy Spirit. May we, as believers, be challenged to overcome our stubborn wills and to live truly obedient and joy-filled lives in Christ.

7
Follow the Leader

John 8:12

One of the odd and rather amusing animal stories I recall from several years back involves a horse named Bailey. It was our daughter's first horse actually, and this story also involves a calf, which she had christened Baby. We had been in Ontario that previous fall and boarded our cows out while we were away. Coming home in December, and having a lot of work to do, we decided to leave the cows till spring. Our daughter brought Bailey home early that following spring, but we still had the cows to bring back. One of the cows had been boarded out to the same family that Bambi had gone to a couple of years earlier. This cow, which we had named Mail-belle was actually Bambi's calf, and had been born on that

Follow the Leader

same farm. We had made the same arrangement with the family in regard to her that we had previously with Bambi. They would keep the cow, with the agreement that the calf would be ours and we would bring it home after it was weaned.

This calf, which would have been Bambi's granddaughter, was the one dubbed Baby by our daughter. She was a Jersey Highland cross with very short and stubby legs. She was black, very hairy, and she was very cute. She also seemed very timid, so we knew she was going to have to be well contained for awhile until she had time to get used to us. We had a difficult time of getting her boarded into the back of the truck and an anxious ride home, but finally we had her situated in her new residence. Then, we had quite the afternoon and evening with 'the little hairy wonder'. My husband and daughter had put her in a pen in the barn until she could get used to her new home. Her stubby little nose barely reached the top of the gate and they even put a beam up blocking the door to make sure she'd stay put. Well, about an hour later, you can imagine our amazement when we looked out and saw 'the Houdini Highlander' standing on the front lawn. After checking the barn we realized that Baby must have jumped over the beam to get out, as it was still securely in place. I couldn't believe that short stubby-legged little beast could possibly have jumped so high.

After we had all spent a fair bit of time trying to round the little bovine up and put her back in the barn, our daughter decided to saddle Bailey and see if she could

Lessons in Farm Life

herd the calf in with her horse. Well, off she went after her and soon they both returned. Oddly enough the calf was not out in front being herded home, she was behind the horse following right along as if it were nothing out of the ordinary for a calf to be playing "follow the leader" with a horse. It was the funniest sight. Baby just seemed to have taken right to Bailey for some reason. After that the calf could be found in the company of that horse as much as possible.

I recall another day that our daughter saddled Bailey up. By this time, we were leaving Baby just inside the fence. Not long after I had seen our daughter disappearing over the hill on her horse, I happened to glance out to find her coming back again, this time not just with Baby in tow, but our dog, Rudy, was also following right along behind them. I guess he didn't want to be left out. At least we could count on Baby staying inside the fence as long as the horse was there, and even if the horse wasn't there, we could count on the calf not being too far away from her.

Thinking back on this unlikely pair made me consider how important it is that we teach our children to be very discerning about choosing the kind of person or people they follow after. It wasn't such a big deal for our daughter's little calf to follow her big horse around. It looked funny and was really amusing and actually a comfort to know the calf would stick close by the horse so we needn't worry about her getting into trouble. However, we do want to caution our children in regard to the kind of friends and role models that they should follow after. It would be a

Follow the Leader

very big deal indeed if they chose to have companions that **would** lead them into trouble, or role models that would encourage them in ways that would be dishonoring to God. By role models I refer to any person, or group, that they may be drawn to and tempted to imitate. In 1 Corinthians 15:33 we find some good advice, *"Do not be deceived: Bad company ruins good morals".* You can not put a bad apple in a barrel of good apples without having the bad apple effect the good ones. More often than not, when a 'professing Christian' chooses to keep company with unbelievers it will be the non-Christians that will be the greater influence rather than the other way around. I'm not talking about friendships, but companion-ships, *"Let no one deceive you with empty words, for because of these things the wrath of God comes upon the sons of disobedience. Therefore do not associate with them; for at one time you were darkness, but now you are light in the Lord.. Walk as children of light (for the fruit of light is found in all that is good and right and true), and try to discern what is pleasing to the Lord"* (Ephesians 5:6-10).

We should certainly be friends with non- Christians, for how could we ever be a witness to them otherwise? However, the bible teaches very clearly we are not to be 'yoked' together unequally. I believe this not only refers to a Christian marrying a non- Christian, but my understanding would be that it also refers to any intimate relationships that could influence us significantly in a spiritual sense, not for the better, but for the worse. This could be a business partnership or a close companionship,

Lessons in Farm Life

"Do not be unequally yoked with unbelievers. For what partnership has righteousness with lawlessness? Or what fellowship has light with darkness? What accord has Christ with Belial? Or what portion does a believer share with an unbeliever" (2 Corinthians 6:14-15)?

As people who think they have only this life to enjoy, unbelievers' goals and ambitions will more likely be focused on self, getting the most out of this life that they possibly can, accumulating as much as possible, for they live only for the here and now. As believers we should be denying ourselves and putting the needs of others ahead of our own. This is a strange concept to our 'me centered' world. We do not want our children to be influenced to focus only on themselves, choosing to seek their own needs, desires, and so forth. This will only lead to covetousness, jealousy and selfish ambition, *"For where jealousy and selfish ambition exist, there will be disorder and every vile practice. But the wisdom from above is first pure, then peaceable, gentle, open to reason, full of mercy and good fruits, impartial and sincere" (James 3:16-17).*

First and foremost we should be teaching our children to follow after Christ, *"Again Jesus spoke to them, saying, I am the light of the world. Whoever follows me will not walk in darkness, but will have the light of life" (John 8:12). "Then Jesus told his disciples, 'If anyone would come after me, let him deny himself and take up his cross and follow me'"(Matthew 16:24).* The call to follow Christ by denying ourselves is one that demands that we completely forsake our natural tendency to look out for our own comfort, power, or fame,

77

Follow the Leader

and that we would live our life with the aim of glorifying God in all that we do.

Getting back to earthly role models, we need to caution our children against listening to the kind of musicians that not only live immoral lifestyles, but reflect that lifestyle within their music as well. Our young people need to be taught the dangers of listening to such music. The kind of music we listen to does influence our thinking. This goes for any kind of entertainment. Young people need to be taught the importance of having the kind of role models that would encourage them to live obedient lives. How can they hope to experience an effective Christian life if they are accepting the kind of entertainment from musicians and actors that would encourage them in an ungodly lifestyle?

As Christian parents we need to be pointing our children to the One and only perfect role model- that is our Lord Jesus Christ. We need to be striving to follow the example of Christ ourselves in order to encourage our children to do the same. As parents, we have to realize the tremendous responsibility we have in this area. Children do, more times than not, even without realizing it, follow in the footsteps of their parents. How often do we find ourselves thinking, "I sound just like my mother?" Others may even tell us, "You looked and sounded just like your mother (or father) right then." As parents, we need to understand that any negative traits we might have can easily be passed on to our children. If our desire is that our children be imitators of Christ, then we must first set

Lessons in Farm Life

the example for them to follow- and strive to be imitators of Christ ourselves. We all sin; we all have negative traits, weak areas in our lives that need to be conquered. We need to be aware of this and determine to be pointing our children to Christ as the Only perfect role model to follow after.

What wonderful promises we are given in the following verses,*"Blessed are those who hunger and thirst for righteousness, for they shall be satisfied" (Matthew 5:6). "Whoever pursues righteousness and kindness will find life, righteousness, and honor" (Proverbs 21:21).* If we are showing our children a hunger for God's word and the difference it makes living our lives in obedience to His Word, then Lord willing, they will follow that example, having a hunger for His word themselves, and a desire to be obedient to it. Of course, we must realize that hunger will not come apart from the working of God's Holy Spirit in their hearts. Understanding this, we must also pray that the Father would draw them unto himself, so that their desire will truly be to imitate the One and only perfect Leader that we, as Christians, should strive to follow after.

8

Restraints and Restrictions

Hebrews 12:9-11

We have a cow by the name of May. Our daughter named her May so she would be able to remember what month she was born in. I call her May-belle because I am more inclined to go with at least two syllable names. May-belle is a pure bred Dexter. She has been my favorite milk cow, mainly because she is the only milk cow that I can remember that didn't swish her tail in my face or attempt to kick over my milk bucket. When I first started milking her last spring, I would always chain her up, as I had our previous milk cows, so that she wouldn't go wandering off on me. Well, after a few weeks of having her chained, and experiencing what a well- mannered and co-operative milk cow she was, I decided to try milking

80

Lessons in Farm Life

without bothering to hook her up. After all, it really wasn't necessary, and all went well-for a few weeks anyway.

However, after a few weeks of being unrestrained, May-belle realized she wasn't restricted to her usual defined little area, and so she started to exert her curiosity. She seemed to be drawn to the pail of water that I always brought out to clean her off with. I don't know why she was so bent on making her way over to this pail and licking the whole outside all over until she finally tipped the bucket, splashing the water and rag inside out on the floor. When she first started edging over in that direction I would just move with her or scold her back into place. However, after an aggravating week or so of trying to keep up with and scolding my very 'well-mannered and cooperative' milk cow, I decided maybe it would be best just to hook her back up again and save myself some aggravation and her a lot more scoldings. The little bit of time it took to do so was well worth the effort in order to keep her within her boundaries. After all, as the old saying goes, "an ounce of prevention is worth a pound of cure."

After mulling over this little scenario, it made me think of the importance of our having specified guidelines for our children to follow and making sure we apply them. Otherwise they might, out of curiosity, end up going places where they shouldn't be going and thereby causing Mom and Dad a lot of aggravation and perhaps earning themselves many a scolding - or worse, if their curiosity happens to lead them into disobedience.

Restraints and Restrictions

We laugh at some of the antics of our children as toddlers. For instance, when one of our older children was in the toddler stage his curiosity led him to upset one of my plants. When I came across him, he was covered in dirt, especially his face and he was evidently thoroughly enjoying himself as he was grinning from ear to ear, with a dirt smeared smile.

When our children grow past this stage of innocent curiosity and into the teen years their curiosity may lead them to more harmful places they should not be going. We do not want our children to follow their curiosity into listening to the type of music, watching the kind of movies or reading the sort of books that would not be appropriate for a Christian young person to listen to, watch or read. We find in *Philippians 4:8 "....whatever is true, whatever is honorable, whatever is just, whatever is pure, whatever is lovely, whatever is commendable, if there is any excellence, if there is anything worthy of praise, think about these things."* It makes it much harder for us to think on 'these things', if we are putting the exact opposite of 'those kind of things' into our minds. Remember the old saying, 'garbage in, garbage out'.

We should also be mindful to prepare our children for any harmful outside influences that are beyond our control. We should not fool ourselves into thinking that we can safeguard our children (even if they are home-schooled) from any and all kinds of harm that may come to them. We need to be aware, too, as they themselves should be, that as they grow older (and, sadly, sometimes

Lessons in Farm Life

even when they are very young) that there are those who may try to take advantage of them in ways that could be very harmful to their physical, emotional, and spiritual well-being. They need to be equipped to handle difficult and varying situations throughout the different stages of their lives.

We also need to teach our children that if they truly know Christ as their Savior, they must remember that God's Holy Spirit lives inside of them, and is with them wherever they go and in whatever they are doing, *"If you love me, you will keep my commandments. And I will ask the Father, and He will give you another Helper, to be with you forever, even the Spirit of truth, whom the world cannot receive because it neither sees him nor knows him. You know Him, for He dwells with you and will be in you" (John 14: 15-17).* So, if their curiosity leads them to an action that is displeasing to God, they are grieving the Holy Spirit, for He is with them in every action they do and even in every thought that they think. Here David implores God to examine his innermost thoughts, searching for the sin in his heart so that He might correct him of it, *"Search me O God, and know my heart! Try me and know my thoughts! And see if there be any grievous way in me, and lead me in the way everlasting" (Psalm 139:23-24)!* Realizing that God knows our every thought should make all of us think twice before making any kind of a decision or even thinking any kind of a thought that would cause the Holy Spirit to be grieved, *"And do not grieve the Holy Spirit*

Restraints and Restrictions

of God, by whom you were sealed for the day of redemption" (Ephesians 4:30).

In Ephesians 6:1, we find this instruction, *"Children obey your parents in the Lord, for this is right."* It is of utmost importance that we teach our children to be obedient above all. What would be the use of having rules and guidelines for them to follow if they are not instilled with the importance of obeying them? It should be understandable that this training needs to begin as early in a child's life as possible. There should be consequences to pay for disobedience, ones that are appropriate to the age of the child, *"Whoever spares the rod hates his son, but he who loves him is diligent to discipline him"* (Proverbs 13:24). In making sure our children suffer the consequences for their disobedience to us as their parents, we are teaching them that they can also expect to suffer consequences for their disobedience to their heavenly Father. A child who is spoiled and not taught the importance of respect and obedience toward his/her parents will likely be one who will pay little attention to the instructions given in God's Word, and will thereby cause him or herself (along with their loved ones), much pain as a result.

We must understand the correct meaning of the word **discipline**, (the older original meaning), which **is; "training that corrects, molds, or perfects the mental faculties or moral character"**. (The more modern definition, which is "to punish or penalize" does not fit with the Bible's teaching). If we are diligent in teaching our children according to God's instructions, training

84

Lessons in Farm Life

them in right behavior that is honoring to God, the hope is that they will adhere to that instruction, thereby saving themselves and their loved ones much pain as a result, *"All scripture is breathed out by God and profitable for teaching, for reproof, for correction, and for training in righteousness, that the man of God may be complete, equipped for every good work" (2 Timothy 3:16).*

I do not remember so clearly the times I'm sure I must have suffered the consequences of my wrong behavior as a child, but I do have a fond remembrance of a time my father showed me grace by not punishing me for my wrong action. I was being foolish and very naughty, and my action had actually been directed toward my brother, however, my father got in the line of fire. As a result, I was sent to my room to await my father's arrival. I was sure I was going to suffer the consequences of my wrong behavior. My dad waited what seemed like a long period of time before following me up the stairs where I sat apprehensively awaiting his arrival. He came into the room, and sat quietly down beside me in order to discipline me. I don't recall his exact words, but I do remember his tone. He spoke to me quietly, and with a gentle tone, reproving me for my naughtiness. Then after receiving an acknowledgment of my wish not to repeat my wrong action, he then gave me a hug and allowed me to go free. I remember experiencing quite a flood of relief as well as thankfulness for the kindness my dad showed to me that day. The grace and mercy we show to our children in those times when they may expect (or deserve) anything

Restraints and Restrictions

but- will long be remembered. This however, does not mean that a child should not suffer the consequences to disobedient and rebellious behavior.

Children should always expect to suffer the consequence of disobedient and rebellious behavior. I would like to caution parents to be careful not to administer punishment to their children in anger. It is with great regret and much shame that I must admit I reacted in anger many times when our older children were in those misbehaving years. I can heartily assure you that you will have a far greater impact on your child when you react to them out of love and concern for their well- being, rather than out of anger at whatever inappropriate behavior they are displaying at the time. We must remember that it is God's kindness that leads us to repentance, as found in Romans 2:4. The child should be disciplined through admonishment or reproof and then *if* punishment is necessary, they must understand it is their own disobedient behavior that leads to that punishment. We should always give an affirmation of our love to our children in such times. If we react in anger toward them, we are not disciplining them, we are only punishing them. When we become angry with our child for their wrong behavior, we need to pray for patience and a calm heart before dealing with whatever unacceptable behavior they are exhibiting at the time, (Galatians 6:1).

It is imperative to give appropriate guidelines for our children to follow, for their well being, both physically and spiritually. For example, if you have a wood burning

Lessons in Farm Life

stove in your home and a toddler running around, you most certainly would teach that youngster to steer clear of that stove, or better still put a guard around it, to prevent real physical harm happening to him or her. As they get older we would be careful to teach the importance of road safety when they are out on their bikes and then move on to all the rules they would need to know and follow in driving a car and so on. There really are a lot of rules and regulations our children are going to have to learn over the years in order to keep them from physical harm.

We also must teach our children to be attentive to the instructions in God's word in order to promote spiritual well-being. Before they are able to read, we can only teach them verbally, but as soon as they can read on their own they should be taught to spend time in God's word daily. It is as important for our children to take in spiritual food as it is they take in physical food. If we neglect to feed our bodies for more than a day even, we will start to become weak and the longer we go without nourishment, the weaker our physical bodies will become. It is the same with our spiritual well being. If we go without the nourishment of God's word for a day, we may feel no ill effects. However, if we neglect to feed our souls on God's word for longer and longer periods of time we will become weaker and weaker spiritually, thereby making ourselves easy prey for the attack of the enemy; *"Be sober-minded; be watchful. Your adversary the devil walks about like a roaring lion, seeking whom he may devour" (1 Peter 5:8).* We certainly do not want ourselves or our children to be easy

Restraints and Restrictions

prey for the devil's schemes. Specific rules and guidelines are most certainly imperative for both the physical and spiritual well- being of our families.

9

Doing Your Duty

Ecclesiastes 12:13

We had been at the Weston farm just three years when we had to have our faithful old collie, Abby, put down because of a tumor. She was fifteen at the time, which is pretty old in dog years, so in lieu of her age, our veterinary friend advised against surgery as it was unlikely that she would survive. She had been with us for nearly 14 years, as we had picked her up at the shelter when she was just over a year old. It was one of the hardest things we had ever had to do, and devastating for our daughter, who was thirteen years old at the time. Abby had been around since before she was born.

By the time Abby had been gone for a few months, we knew we should not put off getting another dog. Our

89

Doing Your Duty

animal- loving daughter was really having a hard time, and missing her a lot. So, my husband took her to the shelter and they brought home a handsome looking Anatolian Shepherd. His name was Rudy. He was not a purebred, but he was a nice looking dog, and he and our daughter took to each other immediately. The day they brought him home, he seemed to settle right in as if he had always been here. It was truly a day to remember. We had been having trouble with the cows getting out, so the day Rudy came home it was no surprise that they happened to be out again. Stepping out of the car, my husband looked at Rudy and pointed to the cows. He said, "That's what you're here for. It's your duty to keep those cows in." Then he gave a holler, "Go, after them! And away he went, barking furiously as he herded them all up. It was really amazing. We would almost have thought he'd done this before. We watched incredulously as he rounded them all up, chased them into the pasture, then came and took his place back beside my husband, looking up at him as if to say, "Duty accomplished, anything else you'd like me to do?" Needless to say he made a very good first impression.

Mulling over the way this particular dog seemed to fit right into his role after being adopted into our family; accepting his duties without any problem whatsoever had me musing over how well we, as professing Christians, do or do not, take to our own roles. We, as believers, have certain duties and responsibilities as a result of our being adopted into the family of God. What a tremendous privilege is ours to receive this adoption, *"In love He*

Lessons in Farm Life

predestined us for adoption through Jesus Christ, according to the purpose of his will, to the praise of his glorious grace, with which he has blessed us in the Beloved" (Ephesians 1:5-6)! When we are adopted into God's family, we are freed from our bondage to sin, no longer enslaved by it, *"But when the fullness of time had come, God sent forth his Son, born of woman, born under the law, to redeem those who were under the law, so that we might receive adoption as sons. And because you are sons, God has sent the Spirit of his Son into our hearts, crying, "Abba! Father!" So you are no longer a slave, but a son, and if a son, then an heir through God" (Galatians 4:4-7).* As sons and heirs of our Heavenly Father, we have certain duties and responsibilities. Hopefully we will be more willing to carry them out than the prophet in the following story.

In the book of Jonah we read about a most unwilling prophet of God. Jonah was instructed by God to go to Nineveh and preach repentance to the people there. Due to the wickedness of the city of Nineveh, Jonah did not feel these people were deserving of God's mercy. So, instead of being obedient and following God's instructions, he set sail for Tarshish. Jonah should have known he could not flee from God's presence. The Lord sent a great wind upon the sea, so great it threatened to break up the ship. Knowing his disobedience was the cause of the storm, Jonah has the men throw him overboard. God graciously saves Jonah by sending a great fish to swallow him up. Jonah remains in this sea creature for three days and nights. At Jonah's repentance, God has the fish cast him

Doing Your Duty

out on the shore. Then, once again, Jonah is told to go to Nineveh and preach repentance to the people. This time Jonah is ready to comply with God's orders, but he did not do so from a willing heart. When the people did actually repent of their sin, causing God to be merciful and withhold the disaster He had warned them about, the Bible tells us that Jonah was exceedingly displeased. He was even angry as he prays to God, *"That is why I made haste to flee to Tarshish; for I knew that you are a gracious God and merciful, slow to anger and abounding in steadfast love, and relenting from disaster" (Jonah 4:2).* How sad, that he felt he was any more deserving of God's great mercy than these people of Nineveh.

We must be ready and willing to do our duty regardless of whether or not it is a pleasant task to which we are called. It may be a very disagreeable or even a boring task. It may even be one for which we would receive no acknowledgement or gratitude. Let us remember that whatever we do, we are to keep in mind that we are serving our Lord through each duty we perform. These duties may come as a result of an exciting or not so exciting career. They may come through the challenging and sometimes mundane tasks of a wife and mother. Whatever the case may be-let us be more willing than the prophet Jonah.

In Exodus we read the account of another unwilling man of God. This passage relates to the time the Lord chose Moses to lead His people out of Egypt. Now Moses was not a good speaker and he was extremely reluctant and unwilling to be God's spokesperson. Coming up with

Lessons in Farm Life

several excuses as to why he would not be a good choice, he tries to reason with God, making particular mention of the fact that he is not eloquent, but slow of speech. God's reply is; *"Who has made man's mouth? Who makes him mute, or deaf, or seeing, or blind? Is it not I, the Lord" (Exodus 4:11)?* Even after God assured him that He would give him the words to say, *"Now, therefore go, and I will be with your mouth and teach you what you shall speak (Exodus 4:12),* Moses still balks at the responsibility God is placing him under.

Here we can learn to trust that God will give us the ability to do whatever task He asks of us, even when we feel we are totally unequipped to perform the duty He requires. However, Moses is still not convinced that he should be the one to take on the tremendous responsibility as God's spokesperson, so he continues pleading to be excused from this task, *"Oh, my Lord, please send someone else" (Exodus 4:13).* God graciously consents to use Aaron, Moses' brother, as Moses spokesperson to the people. God would tell Moses what he wanted Aaron to say, and Moses would relate to Aaron God's messages, so that Aaron, in turn could relay them to God's people.

Unfortunately, we do not have the privilege of God speaking to us audibly today, telling us exactly what he would have us to do. However, we are blessed with his word in which he speaks to us, clearly outlining all of the requirements for those who are his children. If we feel the Lord calling us to an unpleasant task, will we, like Jonah, try to run from our responsibility, or as Moses did, come

Doing Your Duty

up with many excuses not to do as God wishes? He may call us to something as simple as saying, "I'm sorry," and asking someone's forgiveness, or perhaps granting that forgiveness to someone who has offended us. We must be mindful that in our unwillingness to forgive others, neither will God forgive us, *"For if you forgive others their trespasses, your heavenly Father will also forgive you, but if you do not forgive others their trespasses, neither will your Father forgive your trespasses" (Matthew 6:14-15).* Hopefully we will be more aware of our duty, and willing to cheerfully perform the tasks that we are called to.

We find in the book of Genesis a more willing servant of God, as we read the story of Noah, *"Noah was a righteous man, blameless in his generation. Noah walked with God" (Genesis 6:9).* God tells Noah that He plans to destroy the earth because of the wickedness of the people. He wants Noah to build an ark for the saving of his household and of every kind of animal. The ark was to be four hundred and fifty feet long, seventy five feet deep and forty five feet high. God was calling Noah to a tremendous task. This was a project that was to take many, many years. Yet, when God tells him to build this ark and take every kind of animal into it, as well as food for himself and his family, we read of no objections whatsoever. He did not question God as to how he was to complete this enormous task, he just simply obeyed his Lord, *"Noah did this; he did all that God commanded him" (Genesis 6:22). "And those that entered, male and female of all flesh went in as God had commanded him" (Genesis 7:16).* Being a man who walked with God,

94

Lessons in Farm Life

Noah must have realized that God would enable him to complete the task He had called him to. He knew that he served a sovereign God, one who was in absolute control of all things.

Also in Genesis, we read the story of Abraham, who was another of God's willing servants. The Lord tells Abram to leave his family and his country and to go to a land that He will show him. This must have been a very difficult thing to do, to leave the comforts of home and all that is familiar to one and to settle in a foreign land; yet, we read in the twelfth chapter of Genesis, *"So Abram went, as the Lord had told him… Abram was seventy five years old when he departed from Haran" (Genesis 12:4).* And if that was not a hard enough task to comply to, Abraham, after finally being blessed with the son of promise at the age of one hundred, is commanded by God to offer up this son as a burnt offering. We read here in chapter 22, that God is testing Abraham. What a horrendous thing to even contemplate having to do. Yet as we read on in this chapter, Abraham is compliant, even to this unthinkable request. He takes the wood, goes to the place God tells him to, builds the altar, binds his son, lays him on the altar and then, *"Abraham reached out his hand and took the knife to slaughter his son" (Genesis 22:10). "By faith Abraham, when he was tested, offered up Isaac, … his only son, of whom it was said, Through Isaac shall your offspring be named. He considered that God was able even to raise him from the dead" (Hebrews 11:17-19).* What a tremendous relief it must have been to Abraham when the angel of God prevented him

Doing Your Duty

from following through with the killing of his beloved son. When he heard these words, he surely must have praised God, *"Do not lay your hand on the boy or do anything to him, for now I know that you fear God, seeing you have not withheld your son, your only son, from me" (Genesis 22:12).*

In thinking on the faithfulness of these last two men of God, and the unwillingness of the first two, it may cause us to wonder just how faithful we are in performing the tasks that God requires of us. Sometimes the responsibilities we are given may seem overwhelming. However, I doubt they could compare to the duty God gave to Noah in the building of an ark or Abraham's command to sacrifice the beloved son that God had blessed him with in his old age. If we desire to please our Heavenly Father, then we will show our love for him by displaying a heart of obedience toward Him, *"But thanks be to God, that you who were once slaves of sin have become obedient from the heart to the standard of teaching to which you were committed,.." (Romans 6:17).*

As children of God, being adopted into his family, we are called to be holy, giving up the sins of our past, *"As obedient children, do not be conformed to the passions of your former ignorance, but as he who called you is holy, you also be holy in all your conduct, since it is written, 'You shall be holy, for I am holy'" (1 Peter 1:14-16).* We know we cannot be holy, certainly not by our own efforts, nevertheless, we must be striving to live holy lives through the enabling of the Spirit.

Lessons in Farm Life

Let us remember what the whole duty of man is; *"Fear God and keep his commandments, for this is the whole duty of man," (Ecclesiastes 12:13).* If we truly desire from a sincere heart to be obedient and faithful children of our Heavenly Father, then we must spend more time in his word learning all that is required of us as His children. Let us not try to run from our responsibilities, nor give excuses as to why we can't perform them or grumble about having to do them. Let us be willing and compliant, desiring to show our love to our Heavenly Father by our obedience to Him.

10

Submission and Authority

Titus 3:1

The dog that we now have on the Weston Farm is a purebred German Shepherd. She has been with us for approximately two years. Her name is Tia, and she actually belongs to our daughter. Tia is a pretty good dog, fairly obedient, but like most dogs, she does possess her weak points. One day I was setting out to walk over to our good friends and neighbors, in order to get some eggs, as they have their own laying hens. We have been without laying hens for a few years now. Actually I don't think we have had hens since before our faithful old dog, Abby's, time. After Abby and before Rudy came onto the scene, we had first a raccoon, and then a fox, come in and clean up on our chickens. Rudy was a fantastic farm dog as he

Lessons in Farm Life

loved to chase the cows back into the fence when they got out. He was great at keeping any unwanted critters away from the farm, but unfortunately, he had a bad habit of chasing cars as well. Sadly, and to his detriment, he chased one too many cars, which is why we now have Tia.

Getting back to my walk, before I started down the driveway I noticed Tia sitting there with her ears perked up and an eager expression on her face. I knew she wanted to come, but this was not allowed, due to the fact that she liked to keep company with the male dog of one of our other neighbors, and I was not keen on the idea of being surprised with a litter of pups to take care of. Therefore I instructed her very clearly to stay home. So she obediently stayed put- for a few minutes. Then, after I had headed out onto the road from off the driveway and was starting to walk toward my destination, I looked back and noticed her padding along behind. "Tia, No! Go back!" I spoke firmly as I pointed toward home. I could tell she was not happy to comply, as with head down, she slunk slowly back to the house. So, I continued on my way, and after reaching the halfway point, I looked back just to make sure she had stayed put. I didn't see any sign of her, so I completed my journey, feeling confident that she had obeyed my instructions. However, after I got my eggs, and having set foot outside the door, I was disappointed to find this 'fairly obedient dog' peeking guiltily around the corner of the porch. Obviously she had made her way over through the fields, steering clear of the road so I would

Submission and Authority

not see her. I was not impressed and sternly sent her on her way back home.

Mulling over this little incident made me think on the importance of obedience and submission. Now, Tia was definitely not being obedient or submissive. However, since she is just a dog, and does not possess a conscience, I wasn't too terribly concerned with her lack of obedience. It would be nice if she was more obedient, but not as imperative as it is for us, as those who have been created in God's image. We do possess a conscience and should certainly know better. More importantly we have God's Word which teaches us how we are to behave toward those in authority over us and God's word tells us very clearly that we are called to be submissive. In Titus 3:1, Paul exhorts this man in the faith to, *"Remind them* (speaking of the churches) *to be submissive to rulers and authorities, to be obedient, to be ready for every good work."*

Peter encourages us to, *"Be subject for the Lord's sake to every human institution, whether it be to the emperor as supreme, or to governors as sent by him to punish those who do evil and to praise those who do good. For this is the will of God, that by doing good you should put to silence the ignorance of foolish people" (1 Peter 2:13-15).* We should obey those in authority over us, being obedient to the laws of the land in order to commend Christ to others and also to avoid reproach, *"Now who is there to harm you if you are zealous for what is good? But even if you should suffer for righteousness sake, you will be blessed. Have no fear of them, nor be troubled, but in your hearts regard Christ the Lord as holy, always being*

Lessons in Farm Life

prepared to make a defense to anyone who asks you for a reason for the hope that is in you; yet do it with gentleness and respect, having a good conscience, so that, when you are slandered, those who revile your good behavior in Christ may be put to shame. For it is better to suffer for doing good, if that should be God's will, than for doing evil" (1 Peter 3:13-17). Our obedience in this area of submission indicates our willingness to obey God who is the One who is our ultimate authority, *"Let every person be subject to the governing authorities. For there is no authority except from God, and those that exist have been instituted by God. Therefore whoever resists the authorities resists what God has appointed, and those who resist will incur judgment. For rulers are not a terror to good conduct, but to bad" (Romans 13:1-3).*

The only time that we should ever question the authority of those over us, or to actually disobey that authority, is if (or when) that person in authority is clearly acting in violation of scripture. When the high priest questioned Peter and the apostles as to why they were teaching the people in Jesus' name, after they had been instructed not to do so, this was their reply, *"We must obey God rather than men" (Acts 5:29).* We must live in a way that shows our fear of God over men in every instance, regardless of the persecution we may incur as a result. It is to God we will answer one day- not to man.

We are not only to be submissive to those in authority over us, we are also to be submissive to one another regardless of our position, *"submitting to one another out of reverence for Christ" (Ephesians 5:21).* We are to practice

101

Submission and Authority

submission within the church, and inside and outside of the home. Ephesians 5:22 – 6:9 addresses the need for not only wives and children to be submissive, but also slaves and masters. (We could substitute employee and employer in there). This would indicate that we are to be submissive to one another- (within the context of God's word) - regardless of where or who we are. At the end of verse 9 of chapter 6 in Ephesians we are informed that 'there is no partiality' with God.

In Colossians we are given instructions for the family on submission, *"Children, obey your parents in everything, for this pleases the Lord" (Colossians 3: 20)*. We need to teach our children that in their obedience to us as parents, they are showing their willingness to be obedient to God, their Heavenly Father, and in their disobedience toward us, they display an unwillingness to be obedient to their Heavenly Father as well.

"Wives, submit to your husbands, as is fitting in the Lord" (Colossians 3:18). When we fail to comply with this command, it can result in tension and strife within the marriage, thereby causing disruption within the entire family as well. In the third chapter of Genesis we read the account of the fall of mankind. Due to Adam and Eve's disobedience in the garden, the pre-fall harmony and intimacy of their relationship was corrupted by sin. As a result of this, Eve is told that she will experience pain in childbearing and her desire will be for her husband, yet he will rule over her, *"… in pain you shall bring forth children. Your desire shall be for your husband, and he shall rule over*

102

Lessons in Farm Life

you" (Genesis 3:16). This phrase, suggests that her desire is to be in control. This is the natural desire of women in marriages today- unless, by God's grace, the focus of the wife is more toward honoring God through her marriage relationship by her submission to her husband.

I know there are varying opinions as to what exactly is meant by the reference found in scripture to a wife who prays with her head uncovered. I was challenged to look at these verses more closely and consider exactly what Paul was talking about; *"But I want you to understand that the head of every man is Christ, the head of a wife is her husband, and the head of Christ is God. Every man who prays or prophesies with his head covered dishonors his head, but every wife who prays or prophesies with her head uncovered dishonors her head- it is the same as if her head were shaven. For if a wife will not cover her head, then she should cut her hair short. But since it is disgraceful for a wife to cut off her hair or shave her head, let her cover her head. For a man ought not to cover his head, since he is the image and glory of God, but woman is the glory of man. For man was not made from woman, but woman from man. Neither was man created for woman, but woman for man. That is why **a wife ought to have a symbol of authority on her head**, because of the angels. Nevertheless, in the Lord woman is not independent of man nor man of woman; for as woman was made from man, so man is now born of woman. And all things are from God. Judge for yourselves: is it proper for a wife to pray to God with her head uncovered"* (1 Corinthians 11: 3-13)?

103

Submission and Authority

After listening to varying sermons on this subject, I believe Paul is referring to a literal head covering. The Bible is clear when it says the woman ought to have a *symbol of authority* on her head. A symbol is something that is tangible- pointing to something intangible. I believe the head covering is a literal representation of the woman's willingness to be in submission to her husband and therefore to her Lord. The Bible is very clear in verse three where it reads- the head of every man is Christ; meaning Christ is in authority over the man. The Bible is also very clear in that same verse in saying that the head of the wife is her husband; meaning the husband is to be in authority over his wife. When a man prays with his head covered, he dishonors his head, meaning -if he wears a hat in worship, he is showing disrespect to the One who is head over him, which is Christ. When a wife prays without her head covered- with this *symbol of authority,* meaning some form of head covering, which shows her submission to her husband, she is showing disrespect, not only to her husband, but also to God, who has placed her husband in authority over her.

Please note, this is the way I would interpret this passage. I know others may not agree. For some time, I, myself, was firm in my belief that Paul did *not* refer to a literal head covering. Upon my being questioned about this passage, I found myself doing more studying and listening to sermons on both sides of this issue, and in so doing, changing my position on the wearing of

Lessons in Farm Life

head-coverings in worship services. We each must follow our own convictions in regard to this issue.

We are given very clear instructions as to what our conduct should be like within our marriage relationship as wives and we should pay careful attention to it, *"wives, be subject to your own husbands, so that even if some do not obey the word, they may be won without a word by the conduct of their wives- when they see your respectful and pure conduct … let your adorning be the hidden person of the heart with the imperishable beauty of a gentle and quiet spirit, which in God's sight is very precious. For this is the way the holy women who hoped in God used to adorn themselves, by submitting to their husbands" (1 Peter 3:1-5).* In our willingness to be submissive to our husbands, we display an example of how the church is to be submissive to Christ. When we are being disagreeable and uncooperative- it is a clear indication of our lack of submission to God, and our disagreement with His rules. The marriage relationship is to be a picture of the Gospel. It should be a reflection of the church's love for Christ, *"Wives, submit to your own husbands, as to the Lord. For the husband is the head of the wife even as Christ is the head of the church, his body, and is himself its Savior. Now as the church submits to Christ, so also wives should submit in everything to their husbands" (Ephesians 5:22-24).* When we are unwilling to be obedient in this area toward our husbands, it shows our unwillingness to be obedient and submissive to our Lord, for it is He who has very clearly given us these instructions through His Word.

105

Submission and Authority

Just as we teach our children to expect consequences in their disobedience, we too, as wives can expect to suffer consequences when we are disobedient in this area of submission, or any other area of our lives for that matter. I can be very frank and bold in writing on this issue, for it is an area that I struggled with for many years. I can honestly say that not only I, myself, have experienced consequences for my disobedience in this area, but my family has also suffered as a result. We should always be aware of this fact, and teach it to our children, that when we choose to be disobedient to God, that choice has a ripple effect on those around us. Not only will we suffer pain as a result of our disobedience, but our loved ones will suffer pain as well.

Before I go any further I want to make very clear that I am speaking of normal case scenarios here; a man and a wife within a 'Christian' home who are as happily married as possible, given the fact that we are sinners living in a fallen world. God has given us this command not to frustrate us, but for our protection. When I finally came to realize the significance of what these verses were teaching and really determined to become the submissive wife God would have me to be, I found it extremely freeing. It has been such a relief for me to just submit to the headship of my husband, not arguing to get my own way, not manipulating to try to sway his decisions, just a simple letting go. This is not to say that husbands and wives should not discuss matters together, but the husband should have the final say without the wife giving

106

Lessons in Farm Life

him a hard time, even if she may happen to disagree. I firmly believe that God will honor the wife's obedience even if her husband may not be making a wise decision at the time. I have found in situations when I may not agree with my husband, I determine to leave it in God's hands, praying that His will be done. Sometimes my husband will change his mind in these instances and sometimes his decision may remain unchanged. It really doesn't matter. My obedience is not conditional on whether or not I happen to agree with him, or whether I think that God will change his mind. My obedience should not be conditional upon the kind of mood I or my husband may be in at the time either, or on any other circumstance for that matter. My decision to submit to my husband is based on my desire to please and obey my Lord and Savior, and ultimately submit to Him.

Husbands also are given clear instructions here in Ephesians 5:25-30, and in their submission to God in this area they will help to promote a much happier and peaceful home, *"Husbands, love your wives, as Christ loved the church and gave himself up for her, that he might sanctify her, having cleansed her by the washing of water with the word, so that he might present the church to himself in splendor, without spot or wrinkle or any such thing, that she might be holy and without blemish. In the same way husbands should love their wives as their own bodies. He who loves his wife loves himself. For no one ever hated his own flesh, but nourishes and cherishes it, just as Christ does the church, because we are members of his body."* This passage clearly teaches that husbands are

Submission and Authority

to love their wives **sacrificially** just as Christ loves the members of *his* Body-the Church. You are to show love to your wife even if she is having a bad day and is not being very loveable. If your wife is disobedient in the area of submission and tends to fight and manipulate to get her own way, you are still to show love to her. Your obedience in this area also should not be conditional, just as the wife's obedience should not be conditional. Your desire to please your Lord should be stronger than your natural tendency to respond in a negative way to a difficult wife. Perhaps in your obedience in this matter, you will even win her over so that she, too, could find joy in obedience in this area of her life. Then, one day you could rejoice in a wife who, with Proverbs 31 as a guide, is *"far more precious than jewels."*

It should not surprise any of us the tremendous difference obedience in this area can, and will, make within a home. First off, our relationship with our Lord will grow closer, due to our obedience. As a result of this, our relationship with our spouse will grow closer, which will result in closer relationships within the rest of the family as well. Submission is not an easy task in any case, and only by God's grace and through the working of His Holy Spirit in our lives can we attain the goal of submission to all those who are in authority over us, and to one another. However, when we determine by God's grace to be obedient in this area, He will bless us and we will find a true joy in our obedience to Christ. Jesus, our Lord, is the only One who has displayed to us the perfect

Lessons in Farm Life

example of submission- to the will of His Father- that ultimately led Him to his death on the cross on our behalf.

11

Denying Self

Luke 9:23

One day after I had finished filling up the cows' water tub, I stood and watched as the bull and one of the cows came over for a drink. The cow, who had arrived at the tub first, had barely gotten in one swallow before the bull came up from behind and gave her a good shove with his horns, trying to push his way into the tub. I thought to myself, 'How rude.' But then again, what could I expect from a dumb animal?

As I watched while they locked horns, each trying to force the other to go away from the tub, so as to be first to have ones' fill, it made me think of the importance of putting others ahead of ourselves. Now these dumb beasts don't know any better than to push and shove, doing whatever it takes in order to be first or to get their own way. We, however, are clearly taught in God's word the

Lessons in Farm Life

importance of putting others' needs ahead of our own. We need to learn to take the focus off ourselves and put it on God and serving Him by helping to meet the needs of those around us. This is not at all an easy thing to do, especially considering the world we live in, where we are constantly bombarded with messages of self elevation. 'Be good to yourself.' 'You owe it to yourself.' 'You deserve it.' 'Feel better about yourself.' 'Reward yourself.' We live in a very 'me' centered world.

If we, as Christians, are not careful we will be brainwashed by all of these messages that teach us to focus on ourselves. Our focus needs to be on our service to God and helping to meet the needs of others around us. However, it can be so easy to get caught up with the rest of the world in thinking we deserve more and better things. Do we ever find ourselves thinking these kinds of thoughts; "I should have had that promotion", or "I was certain I would have been the one to get that bonus. I'm sure I did a far better job on that assignment." Perhaps we feel we are living a more righteous life and deserve better than others who we feel may not be living in such a way. This is really the world's way of thinking, *"But that is not the way you learned Christ- assuming that you have heard about him and were taught in him, as the truth is in Jesus, to put off your old self, which belongs to your former manner of life and is corrupt through deceitful desires, and to be renewed in the spirit of your minds, and to put on the new self, created after the likeness of God in true righteousness and holiness" (Ephesians 4:20-24).*

Denying Self

We are to put off our old sinful practices, when we once lived only for ourselves, and put on new practices that are befitting a child of God by living in service for Him and others, *"Only be very careful to observe the commandment and the law that Moses the servant of the Lord commanded you, to love the Lord your God, and to walk in all his ways and to keep his commandments and to cling to him and to serve him with all your heart and with all your soul"* (Joshua 22:5). *"For you were called to freedom, brothers. Only do not use your freedom as an opportunity for the flesh, but through love serve one another. For the whole law is fulfilled in one word: You shall love your neighbor as yourself. But if you bite and devour one another, watch out that you are not consumed by one another"* (Galatians 5:13-15).

In Colossians 3 verses 12 through 17 we find these admonishments; *"Put on then, as God's chosen ones, holy and beloved, compassionate hearts, kindness, humility, meekness, and patience, bearing with one another and, if one has a complaint against another, forgiving each other; as the Lord has forgiven you, so you must also forgive. **And above all these put on love, which binds everything together in perfect harmony**. And let the peace of Christ rule in your hearts, to which indeed you were called in one body. And be thankful. Let the word of Christ dwell in you richly, teaching and admonishing one another in all wisdom, singing psalms and hymns and spiritual songs, with thankfulness in your hearts to God. And whatever you do, in word or deed, do everything in the name of the Lord Jesus, giving thanks to God the Father through Him."*

Lessons in Farm Life

That one word 'love' is really the key to living a life that is self- sacrificing, is it not? For we have the perfect example of a self- sacrificing love found in our Lord Jesus Christ who willingly gave up all the riches of heaven to come to earth, to be born as a baby and live as a human in this fallen world, being subject to all that entails. Even more amazing than that, because of His great love, He suffered and died a horrific death on the cross on our behalf, to pay the penalty for our sins, *"There is therefore now no condemnation for those who are in Christ Jesus. For the law of the Spirit of life has set you free in Christ Jesus from the law of sin and death. For God has done what the law, weakened by the flesh, could not do. By sending His own Son in the likeness of sinful flesh and for sin, he condemned sin in the flesh, in order that the righteous requirement of the law might be fulfilled in us, who walk not according to the flesh but according to the Spirit" (Romans 8:1-4).* As those who should be walking according to the Spirit, we must follow in Christ's example by living in service for others *"… whoever would be great among you must be your servant, and whoever would be first among you must be your slave, even as the Son of Man came not to be served but to serve, and to give his life as a ransom for many" (Matthew 20:26-28).*

If we, as professing Christians, do not show love to others, then there is something drastically wrong. The Bible is very clear that it is the display of love through our lives that shows evidence of our belonging to God, *"Beloved, let us love one another, for love is from God, and whoever loves has been born of God and knows God. Anyone*

Denying Self

who does not love does not know God, because God is love. In this the love of God was made manifest among us, that God sent his only Son into the world, so that we might live through him" (1 John 4:7-9). We can find some of the marks of a true Christian in the following verses; *"Let love be genuine. Abhor what is evil; hold fast to what is good. Love one another with brotherly affection. Outdo one another in showing honor. Do not be slothful in zeal, be fervent in spirit, serve the Lord. Rejoice in hope, be patient in tribulation, be constant in prayer. Contribute to the needs of the saints and seek to show hospitality" (Romans 12:9-13).* **"By this all people will know that you are my disciples, if you have love for one another" (John 13:35).** If we are truly filled with the Spirit of God, we will gladly reach out to those around us. For when our hearts are full of the love of God, we will want to share that love with others. It will not be a burden or a chore for us to do so. We will find ourselves actually looking for ways to serve. However, we will not find ourselves doing this if we continue to be focusing on our own desires.

We need to learn to deny ourselves. In the gospel of Luke we are told to take up our cross daily and follow Christ, *"If anyone would come after me, let him deny himself and take up his cross daily and follow me" (Luke 9:23). "And whoever does not take up his cross and follow me is not worthy of me, (Matthew 10:38).* We, in the western world, are really very spoiled; living lives free of physical persecution, lives that are fairly comfortable and full of ease, especially compared with most people in third world countries. How

Lessons in Farm Life

willing are we to be obedient and identify with our Lord-even to the point of death, if need be?

The Bible is very clear on what our focus as Christians should be. In the gospel of Mark, we find one of the scribes coming up to Jesus to ask Him which is the most important commandment, *"Jesus answered, 'The most important is, …you shall love the Lord your God with all your heart and with all your soul and with all your mind and with all your strength. The second is this: You shall love your neighbor as yourself. There is no other commandment greater than these'" (Mark 12:29-31).* In other words, God needs to come first in our lives above all other things and other people. Next to God, we need to learn to put the needs of others ahead of our own. It really is not an easy thing to do; to deny ourselves, to think of others first; putting aside our own comforts and desires in order to meet the needs of those around us. It's so much easier to be self serving, is it not? However, we have not been called to serve ourselves, we have been called to serve one another, therefore, what we need to do is pray for the strength and ability to deny ourselves in order that we may be obedient to this most important command.

12

Is the Grass Really Greener?

Hebrews 13:5

We have had many animals come and go over the past seventeen years, but are now down to just feeding four cows through the winter. Dolly has been the milk cow we have kept the longest having been with us for 8 years now, and we also have her calf, May-belle, whom I hope to be milking in another month or so. Both of them have yearling calves, which I neglected to name, having lost interest in doing so. Actually, I think our daughter refers to them both as Blondie and Dagwood; not terribly impressive cow-like names. Oh well, I don't really have any objections, as the only one I bother to call now is the one I happen to be milking at the time, and I know for certain I won't ever be milking 'Dagwood' and I don't

Lessons in Farm Life

expect to be milking 'Blondie' either. By the time I'm done with milking May-belle, perhaps our youngest son will take over that chore. (?)

I am glad to have fewer animals now as I don't have quite as much energy and enthusiasm that I enjoyed at the beginning of our hobby farm experience. It certainly does make life easier and cuts down on the work load having fewer animals to feed. I am thankful though, for the ones that we do have, as it gives our youngest son a few extra chores to do. Having a hobby farm is a great way to teach youngsters responsibility. He keeps especially busy through the winter months when we are feeding them hay and the barn needs to be kept clean. Usually we would be feeding the large round bales of hay to the cows, but this winter we have used a lot of the small square bales instead, as they were readily available from the stables where our daughter works.

It is so interesting to watch the cows after the flakes of hay are all spaced out among them. They each have their own pile of hay and at first they all munch away contentedly on the pile that is set before them, but after a few minutes, you'll notice one of them gazing over at one of the other piles, then it isn't long before this cow will lumber over pushing the other one out of the way. Then the one whose pile had been stolen will run over and chase another cow from its pile, and so it goes until each one is standing before a different pile than the one she started with. These silly cows are all given exactly the same kind of hay as the others, and the same amount, yet they are

Is the Grass Really Greener?

not content to have what is theirs. They have to go check out the other fellow's. The grass is always greener on the other side of the fence, is it not? Or in this case, the hay is always more tempting in the other guy's pile.

A very good lesson is to be learned from this little scenario. We, as humans are just as guilty as these discontented beasts when it comes to learning to be happy with what we have and where God has put us. It is surely a good lesson for all of us to learn. How often do we look at what our brother or neighbor has, and wistfully wish that we could own as nice a car or as big a house or a better whatever the case may be. When we find ourselves looking at others and wishing ourselves to be in their shoes, we are not only envying, we are coveting what others have. The Bible clearly teaches us in *Exodus 20:17; "You shall not covet your neighbor's house; you shall not covet your neighbor's wife, or his male servant, or his ox, or his donkey, or **anything** that is your neighbor's."* It will only lead to more and more sin, *"You covet and cannot obtain, so you fight and quarrel" (James 4:2).* We are exhorted rather to be content with what we have, *"Keep your life free from love of money, and be content with what you have, for he has said, 'I will never leave you nor forsake you'" (Hebrews 13:5).*

In Philippians 4:11-13 Paul says, *"... I have learned in whatever situation I am to be content. I know how to be brought low, and I know how to abound. In any and every circumstance, I have learned the secret of facing plenty and hunger, abundance and need. I can do all things through Him who strengthens me."* How many of us can honestly say

118

Lessons in Farm Life

that we have learned to be content with whatever God has given us and in whatever situation He Has placed us?

If we are looking at moving from the home we have lived in for several years, and where we have been surrounded by family and friends, to a strange place full of unknowns, as Abraham was, could we be content in such a move? Perhaps we are even called to live in a completely foreign country where we would have to learn a different language in order to communicate. How easy do you think it would be to be content in that situation? Paul said that he had learned to be content wherever he was and in whatever he was doing. We, too, need to learn this kind of contentment, displaying an inner peace at such times, especially in front of our children. We want them to be able to handle difficult situations in a calm and peaceful manner, displaying a complete trust and confidence in God, who is in absolute control over every area of our lives and working all things together for our good.

If our husband were to say to us, "Honey, after we start having our family, I really want you to stay home" and if we were the type of woman who had been enjoying a very fulfilling and prosperous career, could we be content to stay at home looking after our families and keeping house? We need to recall the command given us in scripture; *"Now as the church submits to Christ, so also wives should submit in everything to their husbands" (Ephesians 5:24).* We need also to remember; in obedience, we can expect blessing. Being a stay-at -home mom can be just as challenging (or more so) as being a career woman.

119

Is the Grass Really Greener?

We just need to take that challenge seriously, pursuing our responsibility in the light of scripture.

On that same note, if our husband were to say to us, "I really believe we should consider home-schooling our children as well." Could we be content giving up all the 'free time' it would take to commit to this tremendous task? I use this as an example because this also was an area in which I had many struggles. The first time we heard of home-schooling was well over twenty years ago, before our own children were even of school age. At that time home-schooling was virtually unheard of. I, myself, was not at all keen on the idea, mostly for selfish reasons- no, make that entirely for selfish reasons. I was very much into crafts and painting and really didn't want my 'free time' cut into. However, I could not argue against the fact that spiritually speaking, this would be the best route to take for our children's education. So, begrudgingly, I did endeavor to take on this tremendous task. It was very difficult for the first few years, mainly because of my lack of commitment, not due to the schooling itself. Looking back now, I am so thankful that my husband stuck firmly to this issue of home-schooling. Not that I did such a super job, for I know I could, and should have done far better. However, I do understand and appreciate the value of home-schooling now, much more so today than I did back when we first started.

We, as Christian parents, must realize the enormous responsibility that is ours in the teaching and training of our children to love God and keep His commandments.

Lessons in Farm Life

Our chief end in life should be to glorify God and enjoy Him forever. The greatest commandment we have been given is to love God with all our heart and soul and to love our neighbor as we love ourselves. It is most important that we instill this commandment within the hearts of our children. We need to realize that even more important than encouraging them to pursue a career or to be ready for the responsibilities of marriage and parenthood is that we teach and encourage them to keep the greatest commandment ever given. When we have our priorities in the right place- everything else falls into order as it should, (see Matthew 6:25-34). God first, others next and ourselves last. Our children need to understand the importance of glorifying God in all that they do, regardless of the occupation they choose, whether they lean towards a career in science or medicine, manual labor, missionary work or a stay at home mom. They need to realize that no matter what occupation God calls them to, it is a ministry. For regardless of the occupation that they, or we, ourselves are in, we are to glorify God in and through it, showing a faithful Christian testimony to all those we come in contact with, whether they be members of our own family or fellow co-workers.

When we stop and consider the importance of teaching and training our children in the ways of the Lord, what better way to do so than through their education, as well as through day to day experiences. I wish I had done a better job in teaching our own children the importance of living a Christian world view. However, in order to

Is the Grass Really Greener?

do this, one must live a Christian world-view one's self. Unfortunately, my focus was not on glorifying God in all that I did, not until recent years. Now, I must be content in trying to help our (now grown) children to instill a Christian worldview in the hearts of their little ones. It is so very important that we set the kind of example that we would want our children to follow and in so doing, set the example for generations to follow.

How many of us truly take to heart the verses in Titus 2 where the older women are instructed to teach the young women to, *"love their husbands and children,…. to be …workers at home,…submissive to their own husbands, that the word of God may not be reviled."* We, as older women need to understand the importance of these instructions ourselves, and of acting upon them. We all may be thinking, of course I love my husband and children. However, do we love them as Christ loves, with a sacrificial love? Do we love them enough to deny ourselves, in order to make the kind of choices that would be for their spiritual good? True love is a self sacrificing love, *"Love is patient and kind; love does not envy or boast; is not arrogant or rude. **It does not insist on its own way;** it is not irritable or resentful; it does not rejoice at wrongdoing, but rejoices with the truth. Love bears all things, hopes all things, endures all things" (1 Corinthians 13:4-7).* I truly believe there would be a tremendous impact upon not only our families, but our churches as well, if we, as Christian women, would determine to obey these biblical principles.

Lessons in Farm Life

Perhaps you are a single person and want more than anything to be married. Can you be content in being single as long as God would have you to be, perhaps even for the rest of your life? In 1 Corinthians 7:8-9, Paul says, *"To the unmarried and widows I say that it is good for them to remain single as I am. But if they cannot exercise self-control, they should marry..."* Paul goes on to say in verse 32, *"The unmarried man is anxious about the things of the Lord, how to please the Lord. But the married man is anxious about worldly things, how to please his wife, and his interests are divided."* He then goes on to say the same about the unmarried and married woman as well. This of course is not to say that it is wrong to marry. In verse 38, Paul says that he who marries does well, and he who chooses not to marry also does well. He does, however, give the impression that he actually sees a particular benefit in remaining unmarried.

Now, if we happen to be in the category of those who did marry, as I presume most of us are; speaking to the women here, if our husbands are out of work for a time for whatever reason, or if they need to take a job that pays less, can we be content getting by with less than what we were used to? It would obviously mean we would have to cut expenses. We would have to be more frugal when grocery shopping, or any kind of shopping for that matter. Perhaps our children would have to give up whatever sports or music lessons they were involved in for awhile. Can we teach our children to be content by showing them a good example in refusing to become disgruntled if we are in the position of having to make do with less, *"But if*

123

Is the Grass Really Greener?

we have food and clothing, with these we will be content" (1 Timothy 6:8)? In other words, we need to be content with the basic necessities of life. *If we have what we need, we can be content with that if we choose to be.* The only problem with that is, unfortunately, many times we choose not to be content with that. Our expectations are far too high in this day and age. We need to learn to be content with our basic needs being met, *"Now there is great gain in godliness with contentment, for we brought nothing into the world, and we cannot take anything out of the world. But if we have food and clothing, with these we will be content. But those who desire to be rich fall into temptation, into a snare, into many senseless and harmful desires that plunge people into ruin and destruction. For the love of money is the root of all kinds of evils. It is through this craving that some have wandered away from the faith and pierced themselves through with many pangs" (1 Timothy 6:6-10). "Do not love the world or the things in the world. If anyone loves the world, the love of the Father is not in him" (1 John 2:15).* I don't believe the Bible is teaching us that material possessions are sinful in and of themselves, for it says **the love of money** is the root of all kinds of evil, not money itself. It is when those possessions and a striving after them becomes so important to us that we lose sight of our love for God and the importance of our service to Him and others that we need to be careful.

Another area we may struggle in could be with our appearance. Are we content with the way God has made us? Are we truly happy with our outward appearance? Not that we shouldn't try to keep ourselves fit, for that

Lessons in Farm Life

is important as well. However, do we find ourselves complaining about our figure? Or lack of it? Maybe we are too big or too small. I must admit this is another area that I struggled with for many years. I was never content with my size. Having been the smallest one of my class, from elementary school on I endured the name calling that comes with that position. Then, when the glasses came in fifth grade, I had to endure being branded "four eyes". Having ceased from growing much past the age of 14, I was resolved to being little for life. Now that I am older I don't get teased the way I used to be back in school, but had I been content with the way God made me, I could have just shrugged off those snide remarks, not allowing them to bother me at all. We need to remember that we are His workmanship. He is the one who formed us, making us what we are. We should be content with the way our Creator has made us, *"But now O Lord, you are our Father; we are the clay, and you are our potter; we are all the work of your hand" (Isaiah 64:8).* We need to remember that God is more concerned with what is inside our hearts than our outward appearance, *"For the Lord sees not as man sees: man looks on the outward appearance, but the Lord looks on the heart" (1 Samuel 16:7).* True beauty comes from within, *"… let your adorning be the hidden person of the heart with the imperishable beauty of a gentle and quiet spirit, which in God's sight is very precious" (1 Peter 3:4).*

Can we really learn to be content in any and all circumstances where our Heavenly Father places us? Even though we may not know God's future will for our lives,

125

Is the Grass Really Greener?

we do know his present will and that is the need to be living lives that are, to the best of our knowledge, in accordance with God's word; obedient to the scriptures. We know that we should be content if we are single and we also know we need to be content in our marriage. We need to be content with how God has made us, whatever God has given us, wherever He has placed us, and with whomever He has placed us. In any and all circumstances we are to be content. The question is, can we be???

13

Bawling for Babies

James 3:8-10

It has been a rather noisy place around here since my husband came in the other day, a bit out of breath, and informed me that we had a new calf on the farm. I wasn't terribly excited about the news. After you've had this news time and again for the past several years, it tends to lose some of its former excitement and isn't quite so thrilling anymore. However, I was concerned when he told me that this first- time mother was not behaving in a very motherly way toward her new baby. She was kicking it away and even gave it a bloody nose. He had carried it down to the barn and thankful that May-belle had calved just a few days earlier, I scrounged around for our old milk bottle and nipple. We hadn't used it in years. I wasn't even

Bawling for Babies

sure if we still had it, but I was relieved to see that we did. I then headed down to the barn to milk a few litres out of May. My husband had no trouble getting the little heifer to take the bottle. She seemed quite thirsty. It was a hot and humid day, and the flies were bad, which could have explained the new mother's reaction to giving birth at this time.

The new calf, which I dubbed Molly, (having two heifer calves come within a week of each other, I thought I should give them names to distinguish between them) seemed not to mind that her first feeding came from the hands of humans rather than her mother. Fortunately, we experienced a bit of a shower helping to clear up the bugs and cool the temperature somewhat. My husband put the new mom in the large open pen along with her new baby to see whether she might be more receptive. She still would not let her nurse, but she was displaying some signs of affection toward her new baby, as she gingerly started licking her face. So, we left them alone and thankfully she did allow her baby to nurse before the day was out.

Now instead of just one new mother's complaints to listen to, we now have two. Since we need to spend some time 'calf proofing' the barnyard fence so the calves cannot get out into the main pasture and, from there, onto the road, I have been keeping May-belle's calf (Mindy), in the barn and just letting her mom in a few times a day for feedings. This saves us having to chase the calf all over the place in order to put it in at night. However, when May is

Lessons in Farm Life

outside and away from her baby, she bawls her complaints, letting us know what she thinks of this separation.

We also have to listen to our new 'mom', Blondie, bawl for various reasons. We decided to keep her in the large open pen until we can get the fence dividing the barn area from the main pasture fixed up in order to keep the bull over away from the new mothers. Inside this outdoor pen we have a smaller closed- in pen where Molly tends to spend a fair bit of time. Now that her mom has decided she wants her baby around after all, and she wants her close by at all times, she bawls and bawls when Molly goes inside this little pen because she is unable to fit into it herself. I don't know if she is bawling at her baby to come out or if she is bawling because she, herself can't go in. Either way, she is very vocal in her complaints. So, we have May-belle bawling for her baby, and Blondie bawling at her baby, and we are showered with the complaints of these 'bawling bossies' at various times throughout the day and night. It will be nice when we get them all into a settled routine so we won't have to listen to their bawling anymore and can enjoy some peace and quiet around here once again.

Chuckling over the way these new moms are so vocal in voicing their complaints got me thinking how sometimes we, as Christians, can be pretty vocal in a negative way ourselves. The sounds of our complaints are no more pleasant than these bossies bawling for their babies. Yet, we should be better able to control our

Bawling for Babies

complaining than these bawling beasts. Unfortunately, a lot of times we don't exercise that control.

We actually need to maintain better control over our tongue in every way and in all occasions that we use it. Our tongue is a very small part of our body, but it is one we at times seem to have the least control over, and it is also the one that gets us into the most trouble, *"For we all stumble in many ways, and if anyone does not stumble in what he says, he is a perfect man, able also to bridle his whole body" (James 3:2). "So also the tongue is a small member, yet it boasts of great things" (James 3:5). "…no human being can tame the tongue. It is a restless evil, full of deadly poison. With it we bless our Lord and Father, and with it we curse people who are made in the likeness of God. From the same mouth come blessing and cursing. My brothers, these things ought not to be so" (James 3:8-10).*

How often do we find ourselves complaining to others about our husband/wife, or our children - or anyone else for that matter? It is so easy to see the faults in others. I know I have found myself at times listening to a particular sermon and thinking, "I hope so and so is paying attention to this and learning from it. This is a really good message for him (or her)." We need to be careful to apply God's word to our own hearts, for we are responsible for our own actions, not the actions of those around us.

We need also to be mindful as parents that our children take note of, not only the way we treat them, but of the way we treat one another. Let us be careful as wives not to use our tongues to criticize our husbands and as

Lessons in Farm Life

husbands not to be critical of our wives. For we are setting an example for our children to follow and by this example, we are setting the stage for the way our children will speak of us and to us, as well as to their future spouses. We should show respect for one another, teaching them, in turn, to be respectful to us as their parents. It is very important that our children are taught to respect and honor their parents. In Leviticus 19:3, we are told; *"Every one of you shall revere his mother and father."* The honor and reverence of parents was very important back in Old Testament times; *"Cursed be anyone who dishonors his father or his mother"(Deuteronomy 27:16).* God shows us through his word that it is still very important today, *"Children, obey your parents in the Lord, for this is right. Honor your father and mother (this is the first commandment with a promise), that it may go well with you and that you may live long in the land," (Ephesians 6:1-3).* Children must understand that these commands are given for their protection. Regardless of whether our children are speaking of, or speaking to their parents, or anyone else who is older than they are, they need to be taught to do so in a tone and a manner of respect. It will save them a lot of hardship down the road-if they exercise their will to obey this important command.

The use of our tongue can also be to our downfall in that we may be 'talking the talk' of a Christian, yet not 'walking the talk'. We may be like the Pharisees of Jesus' day who maintained a religious lifestyle, yet their hearts were far from God, *"....God, I thank you that I am not like*

Bawling for Babies

other men....(Luke 18:11). This man obviously did not have the right understanding of where his heart was with God or his own sinfulness. It is really a rather frightening thought when we consider there are many people out there who maintain a religious lifestyle, and go through many of the motions of living a 'Christian' life, yet they are really just fooling themselves. They fit the description of the Pharisees in many ways. The Pharisees were not terrible people; they were very moral and upright citizens, going through all the outward motions of living a righteous lifestyle. However, their hearts were far from God, *"Woe to you, scribes and Pharisees, hypocrites! For you are like whitewashed tombs, which outwardly appear beautiful, but within are full of dead people's bones and all uncleanness. So you also outwardly appear righteous to others, but within you are full of hypocrisy and lawlessness" (Matthew 23:27-28).* These men of Jesus' day were 'talking the talk,' they knew all the right things to say and were saying them, (for the most part); they were very involved in religious activities; *but*, they were relying on their own righteous deeds to get them into heaven. They were just fooling themselves. Here we find Jesus talking again to the Pharisees; *"Well did Isaiah prophesy of you hypocrites, as it is written, 'This people honors me with their lips, but their heart is far from me; in vain do they worship me, teaching as doctrines the commandments of men.' You leave the commandment of God and hold to the tradition of men" (Mark 7:6-8).* Let us be wary, making sure the words that we speak do not contrast with a heart that is actually far from God.

Lessons in Farm Life

Our tongues need to be used for good and not for evil, for building up, not tearing down, *"Whoever desires to love life and see good days, let him keep his tongue from evil and his lips from speaking deceit; let him turn away from evil and do good; let him seek peace and pursue it" (1 Peter 3:10-11).* We need to be mindful that others are watching us, listening to the things that we, as professing Christians, are saying. Are we careful in our speech, that we not offend others or dishonor our Lord through our conversation, *"I will guard my ways, that I may not sin with my tongue; I will guard my mouth with a muzzle," (Psalm 39:1)?*

In thinking of the tremendous harm the tongue can do, I am reminded of something I heard in a sermon given by Alistair Begg on 'Words'. In it we were reminded of three things that cannot come back; 1) the spent arrow, 2) the spoken word, and 3) the lost opportunity. If we would stop and consider the potential for harm of the words that we are about to utter, perhaps we would be more careful to 'guard our mouths with a muzzle'. This little piece of muscle within our mouths can destroy a relationship, ruin a friendship, and harm a person's character; essentially it can wreak all kinds of havoc within a very short span of time, *"How great a forest is set ablaze by such a small fire! And the tongue is a fire, a world of unrighteousness. The tongue is set among our members, staining the whole body, setting on fire the entire course of life, and set on fire by hell" (James 3:6).*

Do we ever stop and consider the pain that may be caused by the words that we speak, *"There is one whose rash words are like sword thrusts, but the tongue of the wise brings*

Bawling for Babies

healing" *(Proverbs 12:18)?* We find David speaking here in Psalms at the time he is fleeing from Saul, *"My soul is in the midst of lions; I lie down amid fiery beasts- the children of man, whose teeth are spears and arrows, whose tongues are sharp swords" (Psalm 57:4).* This little red wagging thing within one's mouth can indeed cause a great deal of damage. We need to strive to be using our words to heal and not to harm. Here we find Paul writing to the Corinthians, *"For I fear that perhaps when I come I may find you not as I wish, and that you may find me not as you wish- that perhaps there may be quarreling, jealousy, anger, hostility, slander, gossip, conceit, and disorder. I fear that when I come again my God may humble me before you, and that I may have to mourn over many of those who sinned earlier and have not repented ..." (2 Corinthians 12:20-21).* All of these troubles are caused by the tongue, are they not? We quarrel with our tongue, we show jealousy by our words; our anger is displayed by the things that we say and in the tone that we say them; hostility also can be shown through the use of our tongue. We sin through our conversation when we gossip about others. We slander another person's character by the unkind things we say about them, things we do not even know for certain to be entirely truthful, and conceit inevitably comes from our boasting.

All of these things bring about disorder within our Christian lives. Let us be careful to use our tongues in a way that would be glorifying to our Lord, in order to bring Him praise and honor. We do not want to grieve the Holy Spirit by the use of our tongue, *"Deliver me from*

Lessons in Farm Life

blood-guiltiness, O God, O God of my salvation, and my tongue will sing aloud of your righteousness. O Lord, open my lips, and my mouth will declare your praise" (Psalm 51:14-15). Our only hope of taming this potential for destruction is to be found in the grace and strength of our Lord, through the working of His Holy Spirit within our lives, *"Teach me to do your will, for you are my God! Let your good Spirit lead me on level ground" (Psalm 143:10)!* We need to keep our focus on our Lord, for He alone can keep us steadfast and help us to use our tongues for the purpose they were intended, *"I saw the Lord ever before me, for he is at my right hand that I may not be shaken; therefore my heart was glad, and my tongue rejoiced, my flesh also will dwell in hope" (Acts 2:25-26).* May we look to our Lord to put a guard over our mouth, so that we would be more inclined to use our tongues, not for evil, but for good, and for the glory of our great and loving Lord.

14

Be on Your Guard

Ephesians 6:10-18

This past week has been filled with early morning frustrations for my husband and I as we try to get May-belle back into the routine of coming into the barn each morning to be milked. Not having been milked all winter makes this a challenging task. My once 'well mannered and co-operative' cow is not so, at the present time. We have been getting up at 6:30 each morning to go out, bring May in and hook her up so I can clean her off, give her some grain, and then try to milk her. She has been pulling and tugging on her chain each morning, stopping briefly to eat some grain, then going back to pulling and tugging, as well as moving forward and backward, making it very difficult for me to try and milk her.

Lessons in Farm Life

I decided to go out before my husband this particular morning as he had a few nights in a row of very little sleep, and was having a hard time getting moving. I actually went out, brought May-belle into the barn and went through the whole routine without nearly the fuss we'd been having the past several days. My husband came into the barn as I was finishing up and I was pleased to be able to tell him that everything had gone fairly smoothly for me this morning. However, I spoke too soon, as the next step I was about to take would completely burst my big bubble of confidence.

Since I was feeling so pleased with myself, and quite confident that I would now be able to handle this early morning ritual on my own, I reached over to let the calf out of its pen- without realizing that I had neglected to close and hook the gate leading out of the barn. I guess I should not have been surprised that Mindy, after being shut in the barn all week, rather than going for her breakfast, made a bolt for the door before I could even turn around. I guess she was feeling keener on having her freedom than on having her food. She zoomed out of the open doorway like a shot, into the wide spaces beyond. Needless to say I was very dismayed at my carelessness. I wailed to my husband, "I can't believe I did that." He was not at all perturbed by the situation. I'm so thankful for such a patient and easy-going spouse. We did try and get her in, but ended up making matters worse as she found her way through a couple of boards in the fence and gained even more freedom in the main pasture. So, we came in,

137

Be on Your Guard

leaving her to find her way back over to her mom on her own. After breakfast and devotions, my husband headed off to work. Mindy did eventually find her way back over to her mom, so my son and I went out to block off as many areas as we could find that might become escape routes for her. He then suggested we herd her back in the barn, which we did, without too much trouble. Thankfully, our early morning adventure was over and so we then returned to the chores we had allotted for that day. I determined not to be so careless next time. After this I will certainly be more on my guard.

Musing over the foolishness of my negligence in this early morning fiasco, allowing myself to become over confident and so letting down my guard, made me think on the importance of 'being on our guard' as Christians. When we think of one being on guard, often the position of a soldier would come to mind. And so it is that we, as Christians, are likened to soldiers of Jesus Christ, *"Share in suffering as a good soldier of Christ Jesus" (2 Timothy 2:3).* As soldiers of Christ we must be alert, always on the lookout for danger. In God's word we are admonished to put on the armor of God so we may be prepared to fight off the attacks of the enemy, *"… Be strong in the Lord and in the power of His might. Put on the whole armor of God, that you may be able to stand against the schemes of the devil. For we do not wrestle against flesh and blood, but against the rulers, against the authorities, against the cosmic powers over this present darkness, against the spiritual forces of evil in the heavenly places. Therefore, take up the whole armor*

138

Lessons in Farm Life

*of God, that you may be able to withstand in the evil day,
and having done all, to stand firm. Stand therefore, having
fastened on the belt of truth, and having put on the breastplate
of righteousness, and as shoes for your feet, having put on the
readiness given by the gospel of peace. In all circumstances take
up the shield of faith, with which you can extinguish all the
flaming darts of the evil one; and take the helmet of salvation,
and the sword of the Spirit, which is the word of God, praying
at all times in the Spirit with all prayer and supplication. To
that end keep alert with all perseverance, making supplication
for all the saints, ..." (Ephesians 6:10-18).*

Any soldier who would go out to battle without being
fully- equipped and wearing his armor would be very
foolish. He would not last long on the battle-field without
the protection that his armor provides. It is the same with
the Christian soldier as well. We would not do well in our
daily lives as we struggle against the many temptations to
sin, trying to fight off the attacks of our enemy, the devil.
Striving not to give in to our own sinful desires, without
the aid of our armor; the belt of truth, the breastplate of
righteousness, the shield of faith, the helmet of salvation
and the sword of the Spirit, which is the word of God,
would be very difficult, indeed. As good soldiers of Christ,
we *must* be properly equipped.

In regard to our Christian walk, we need to faithfully
strive to follow and obey the commands given us within
our guidebook, the Bible. When we fail to follow these
guidelines, we will become stumbling blocks to others,
and it is a very serious matter when we are the occasion

Be on Your Guard

for one who is either new to, or weaker in the faith to fall. The Bible describes to us just how serious an offense this is, *"But whoso shall offend one of these little ones which believe in me, it were better for him that a millstone were hanged about his neck, and that he were drowned in the depth of the sea. Woe unto the world because of offenses! For it must needs be that offenses come; but woe to that man by whom the offense cometh" (Matthew 18: 6-7)!* This is another reminder of the importance of examining ourselves daily in the light of God's word, and of praying for the grace needed to live faithful consistent lives that we would be true testimonies of ones who claim to follow Christ.

Another danger we may encounter could be that of false teachers. We may have many opportunities to listen to the preaching of God's word by various teachers and preachers. As we do so, we must be on guard against false teaching; able to listen to the preaching of God's word and discern between what is true and what is false. In order to do this, we need to spend time reading God's word, studying it, and praying for a right understanding of what it contains, *"And many false prophets will arise and lead many astray" (Matthew 24:11).* These men may be very convincing, so we must always be on our guard, for they are what the Bible refers to as ones who pose as 'angels of light,' but are used by the devil to bring about divisions within the church, *"…Even Satan disguises himself as an angel of light. So it is no surprise if his servants, also, disguise themselves as servants of righteousness" (2 Corinthians 11:15).* We need to be able to distinguish between the minister

140

Lessons in Farm Life

of God's Word who truly has a heart for the gospel and a love for God's people, and one who has merely taken this position of 'minister' without really understanding exactly all that entails. Some 'men of the word' have even been known to say they would find another occupation if they thought they could find one that paid as well and enabled them so much free time. These are obviously not men who understand what a high calling it is to take on the role of 'shepherd' over the flock of God. They do not have a heart for God, or his people.

One clear way to tell if a man who ministers God's word is genuine in his motivation to do God's will, would be to look for the fruit in his life. The Bible tells us we will recognize those who are counterfeit shepherds by their fruits, *"Beware of false prophets, who come to you in sheep's clothing but inwardly are ravenous wolves. You will recognize them by their fruits" (Matthew 7:15-16).* We should be able to discern if a pastor's motivation for performing his duties comes from a heart of love and a faith that is sincere. In 1 Timothy 1:3-4, we find Paul instructing Timothy; *"As I urged you when I was going to Macedonia, remain at Ephesus that you may charge certain persons not to teach any different doctrine, nor to devote themselves to myths and endless genealogies, which promote speculations rather than the stewardship from God that is by faith."* Paul goes on to say; *"**The aim of our charge is love that issues from a pure heart and a good conscience and a sincere faith.** Certain persons, by swerving from these, have wandered away into vain discussion, desiring to be teachers of the law, without*

141

Be on Your Guard

understanding either what they are saying or the things about which they make confident assertions" (1 Timothy 1:5-7).

Some pastors may be preaching correctly, but not understanding or applying their teaching to their own lives. In other words they may be dishing out some good meat (spiritually speaking), yet not partaking of it themselves. It would put one in mind of that old saying in reference to a parent and child relationship where the parents may be trying to encourage their child to do something that they are unwilling to do themselves. So, of course the child may challenge the parent on this and then comes the saying, "Do what I say, not what I do." Our pastors should be striving to imitate Christ as an example to their congregations, in the same way a parent needs to strive to imitate Christ as an example for his/her children to follow. We need to pray for our pastors regularly that they would be faithful stewards of God's Word, and living examples of it, diligently seeking the help of God's Holy Spirit as they prepare each sermon. If they do not show that they have the heart of a shepherd by the way they intermingle with their flock, we need to be praying that God would instill within them the heart of a servant, likened to the heart of the only true 'Shepherd'. May they even be as Ezra the priest was, *"... for the good hand of his God was on him. For Ezra had set his heart to study the Law of the Lord, and to do it and to teach his statutes and rules..." (Ezra 7:10).* Ezra obviously had a right understanding of who God is and his duty toward Him.

Lessons in Farm Life

Those in charge of feeding the flock of God need to remember they are serving the God of the universe; a holy and perfect God, the King over all. If we were to serve in the palace of an earthly king, and were in charge of feeding his royal family, what kind of food would we be likely to dish out to our master's kin? We would certainly not be feeding them something we just threw together to save time, nor would we feed them leftovers or anything of inferior quality. The king would be expecting only the best of food for his royal family. So it is with our Lord. He expects his servants to be dishing out only the best that they can give. The only way for them to do this is to allow themselves to be guided in the truth of God's word through the help of the Holy Spirit. In John 21: 15 -17, we find evidence of Christ's concern for the feeding of His sheep, *"When they had finished breakfast, Jesus said to Simon Peter, 'Simon, son of John, do you love me more than these'? He said to him, 'Yes, Lord, you know that I love you.' He said to him, 'Feed my lambs'. He said to him a second time, 'Simon, son of John, do you love me?' He said to him, 'Yes Lord: you know that I love you.' He said to him, 'Tend my sheep.' He said to him the third time, 'Simon, son of John, do you love me?' Peter was grieved because He said to him the third time, Do you love me? And he said to him, 'Lord, you know everything; you know that I love you.' Jesus said to him, 'Feed my sheep'."* Why would Jesus have repeated Himself three times? Perhaps it had something to do with Peter's denial of Jesus three times. Perhaps it may have been in part for emphasis sake, because we are such forgetful

143

Be on Your Guard

hearers. We are far more likely to remember something if it is repeated two or three times rather than just once. We know the importance of feeding Christ's Church is a very great responsibility. We also know that sheep is used as a metaphor for the church. If one has the responsibility of feeding the flock of God, it is imperative that he take seriously the responsibility placed upon him- taking the time to prepare each meal properly, following the Master's instructions carefully, and serving the meal in such a way as to display his love for the One he is in service for.

We really need to be discerning as we listen to those who speak God's word, mindful that the man who stands behind a pulpit each Sabbath day morning is not infallible. He may claim to speak upon God's behalf to his people, yet he may not be doing so for the right motivation. If a pastor truly has a heart for the gospel, it should show in his teaching, as he preaches the *whole* counsel of God. When a pastor feels there is an area lacking in the understanding of some within the congregation, if his theology is correct(in believing in a Sovereign God who is in complete control over *every* area of our lives), he will pray about that and continue to preach the whole counsel of God. He will trust God to do the work that needs done to open the understanding of the ones he feels are struggling to accept certain truths. He will not become frustrated and upset at *his* being unable to make his parishioners come to that understanding, because he will realize that *only* His Sovereign God can open their eyes to the right understanding of his word.

Lessons in Farm Life

However, if his theology is off and he is *not* looking to a Sovereign God, then he will take it upon himself to preach on the area of concern, usually to the detriment of the full counsel of God. His actions show that he believes that he wants to, and even *can* work this change himself, rather than trusting in God to do the work. When we feel that we can take it upon ourselves to change the thoughts and ideas of others in regard to their understanding of God's word, we are displaying signs of pride, putting ourselves in the place of God and robbing God of His glory, *"I charge you in the presence of God and of Christ Jesus, who is to judge the living and the dead, and by his appearing and his kingdom: preach the word; be ready in season and out of season; reprove, rebuke, and exhort, with complete patience and teaching, (2 Timothy 4:1-2)."*

It shows an imbalance in the preaching when pastors tend to focus their teaching in one area alone. Some will preach consistently on the responsibility of man to the neglect of preaching on the Sovereignty of God, while others will focus their preaching on the Sovereignty of God while neglecting to preach on the responsibility of man. **God is 100% Sovereign, *yet* man is also 100% responsible**. There must be an equal balance of both in the preaching of the Word. Here we have Paul speaking in *Acts 20:26-27, "Therefore I testify to you this day that I am innocent of the blood of all of you, for I did not shrink from declaring to you the whole counsel of God."*

Paul's ministry in Ephesus was both public and private as he even spent time in the homes of his flock, *"I did not*

145

Be on Your Guard

shrink from declaring to you anything that was profitable, and teaching you in public and from house to house, testifying both to Jews and to Greeks of repentance toward God and of faith in our Lord Jesus Christ" (Acts 20:20). We are given a clear picture of Paul's burden for his flock in verse 31, *"Therefore, be alert remembering that for three years I did not cease night or day to admonish everyone with tears" (Acts 20:31).* This certainly shows us a good illustration of a pastor who desired to have a heart like the true 'Shepherd;' one with a burden for *every* one of his flock, not just the few who tend to be more involved in the ministry of the church, or those he may have more in common with, *"My brothers show no partiality as you hold the faith in our Lord Jesus Christ, the Lord of glory.... But if you show partiality, you are committing sin and are convicted by the law as transgressors" (James 2:1, 9).*

A pastor should be one who shows a burden for all of his people, and this should show through his preaching of the full counsel of God, through his visitation, through his compassion for the grieving, guiding of the wayward and the careless; in other words carrying out all of his duties through his love for Christ and the love he has for his congregation. Now, of course, if a pastor happens to have a very large congregation, it would be impossible for him to visit each family. This is where the role of the elders comes in. The elders should actually carry out this duty of visiting families within a small congregation as well; they should visit the people regardless of the church's size, especially the sick and those who are new in the faith or

146

Lessons in Farm Life

wayward in their ways. However, there would certainly need to be more elders actively carrying out these duties within a larger congregation, where it would be more difficult to know so many of the people on a more intimate basis.

If we have a burden upon our heart, we should be able to feel confident in taking it to our pastor or one of our elders, knowing that we will receive guidance from the scriptures, and trusting that they will respond to us through love and concern for our spiritual well-being. Unfortunately, some pastors may try to influence us in a way *they* feel would be in our best interest without really searching the scriptures and praying for godly wisdom in dealing with the situation at hand. We must learn to discern between those who think they are acting in our best interests and those who are clearly giving godly counsel. If we do not know what God's word is saying to us, then we will not be on our guard against those who will try and lead us down the wrong path. We need to be wary of any kind of counsel given us, whether it come from a pastor or even a friend with very good intentions. We want to be careful to follow counsel that would be in accordance with God's word.

A very good example of the importance of being on our guard in this way is found in 1 Kings Chapter 13. Here we read the account of the man of God from Judah who is sent to confront Jeroboam, king of Israel at that time, about his cultic practices. He is commanded by God not to eat or drink while he is there, nor to return home

Be on Your Guard

by the way that he came. He clearly tells Jeroboam he will not refresh himself when he is issued an invitation, for he would be disobeying God's commands in so doing.

However, later on we find another prophet who lived in Bethel, an older man whose sons had informed him of all the former prophet's words. This second man finds out which way the man from Judah had gone and goes after him. In finding him he invites him to come home to eat bread with him. After the man of God tells him he may not eat or drink nor return home the same way that he came, the older prophet tells him that he also is a prophet and an angel had spoken to him by the word of the Lord telling him to bring the prophet from Judah home with him that he may eat bread and drink water. This older prophet was lying, for the Lord had certainly not given him any such instructions. However, the man from Judah naively believes him, and so accepts the invitation from the older prophet. We do not know the motivation of this older man's falsehood, but it would certainly appear that it was selfish in nature. He may have wanted to get to know this man of God from Judah or perhaps he really felt he was acting in this man's best interests, thinking he should have some nourishment before beginning his journey home. I don't believe we could suggest that God had sent the older prophet to the man of Judah for the purpose of telling a falsehood in order to test his faithfulness, for our Holy God does not tempt us to sin, *"Let no one say when he is tempted, "I am being tempted by God," for God cannot be tempted with evil, and he himself tempts no one.*

Lessons in Farm Life

But each person is tempted when he is lured and enticed by his own desire. Then desire when it has conceived gives birth to sin and sin when it is fully grown brings forth death" (James 1:13-15). However, God does test our obedience when we are confronted with the temptation to sin. Unfortunately this man of God from Judah failed the test, for he should have realized that this older prophet's instructions were in clear violation of his own orders from God. In his disobedience to God's word the man from Judah suffers dire consequences, *"Because you have disobeyed the word of the Lord and have not kept the command that the Lord your God commanded you, ... your body shall not come to the tomb of your fathers" (1 Kings 13:21-22).* As we read on in the story we find that the man of Judah is met by a lion on the road and killed. This is a very sobering reminder that there are consequences to pay for our disobedience to God. So, we too, must be very careful in believing everything that we are taught or told just because a 'man of God' is doing the teaching or telling. For these men of God are human as we are, with the same weaknesses and temptations to sin. We should certainly give them the respect due to them. However, we are not to place them upon a pedestal.

We do hope and pray that our pastors would be diligent in their study of God's word and seeking the help of His Holy Spirit as they prepare sermons, and as they give counsel to others. However, unless we ourselves study God's word and pray for a right understanding of it, we cannot be sure that what we are being taught is always in accordance with it, *"Beloved, do not believe every spirit, but*

Be on Your Guard

test the spirits to see whether they are from God, for many false prophets have gone out into the world" (1 John 4:1). Let us be like the men of Berea who searched the scriptures daily to see if what they were being taught was really true, *"Now these Jews were more noble than those in Thessalonica; they received the word with all eagerness, examining the scriptures daily to see if these things were so" (Acts 17: 11).*

We need to be on our guard against the attack of the enemy, alert to those who are false in their teaching, and studying diligently with much prayer for a right understanding of God's word. Let us be faithful, not only as we examine the scriptures each day, but also in the examination of our hearts, testing to see if we are truly living each day in accordance with those Holy Scriptures.

15

Equipped for the Task

Psalm 78:5-7

It has been several weeks since the birth of Mindy and Molly and we still keep them both contained in separate pens. Molly is in the larger outside pen, with a smaller pen attached that is closed in and dry so she can get in out of wet weather. Mindy has been in the barn all this time. She has free reign of the barn, but it is not very big, so that she really can't do much running around, not like Molly can in the outside pen. It has always bothered me that Mindy doesn't enjoy as much freedom as Molly, so one morning I decided that I should start putting Mindy over with Molly in the outside pen, just during the day. I would put her back over in the barn at night as she is still being nursed by May-belle. I was quite pleased with my

Equipped for the Task

idea, thinking how happy Mindy would be to be able to run around outside for the day.

Deciding I needed something to use as a collar, I rooted around and came across one of our daughter's old horse halters. I wasn't sure how I was going to get it on her, but I did manage to slide one part over her head, (after chasing her all over the barn for about ten minutes). Of course the rest of it just hung down, looking rather silly, but I'm sure she didn't mind. I then took a dog leash and hooked it onto the halter. There, I figured I was all set. This won't be so hard now. After all, Mindy is only 6 weeks old. However, I decided to tie the leash around my waist just to be certain that she wouldn't get away on me. I wonder if any of you have any idea how much strength a small 6 week old calf really has? Well, I was about to find out.

I had barely set foot outside the barn door with Mindy before realizing that maybe this wasn't such a good idea after all. I was thankful that the barn- yard wasn't too wet and mucky, for, had it been, I would have been as well. That 'little' Dexter calf took me for quite a ride. It wasn't far from the barn to the pen, but it took us a *long* time to get there. Huffing and puffing, I was pretty worn out by the time I had dragged Mindy in through the gateway to the open pen. I quickly unhooked the leash and let her go. She nearly came through the cage wire on the gate. I decided I had better do some reinforcing to the pen before I left her unattended. So, after adding some more boards to be sure she wouldn't try to escape, I went to rest my

152

Lessons in Farm Life

wobbly knees, having decided that I wasn't going to be the one to put her back in the barn again after supper. I was quite grateful to be able to hand over that chore to my husband, who was a lot stronger and more capable of handling the little tornado than I. I haven't felt nearly so sorry for her since then, and I was definitely not going to argue with my husband when he told me he didn't think it was a good idea to be putting the calves together through the day. After that morning's adventure I was quite ready to agree.

As I was resting up and recalling my morning adventure, it made me think on the importance of being properly equipped to take on any kind of challenging task. With regard to our Christian lives, this could be anything from raising our children to restoring a broken relationship. It really is of utmost importance to be properly prepared to take on any challenging task that is put before us.

When I think on the importance of being properly equipped in the raising of our children, it makes me ponder over Daniel's circumstance in being exiled to Babylon as a young man, probably just in his teens. He must have had very godly parents who had raised their children in the ways of the Lord, teaching and training them in all aspects of life. If he had not been firmly grounded, and understanding the truth of God's word through the work of the Spirit, how could Daniel have failed to succumb to the Babylonian's brainwashing? He couldn't have. It is not an easy task to live in such a way as to avoid conforming

Equipped for the Task

to this world. Daniel shows us a very good example of one who did fulfill this very task in his day; and he did so by continually seeking God's help. I would encourage the reading of the first 6 chapters of Daniel for illustrations of this man's faithfulness in the midst of many difficult and trying circumstances. He remained faithful to God throughout the whole of his life as he lived it in exile. It made me wonder if our children would hold up under such conditions. Have we even equipped them to live a Christian worldview, whether they are being educated within the public school system, Christian school or home schooled?

A very familiar proverb comes to mind when we think of the teaching and training of our children, *"Train up a child in the way he should go; even when he is old he will not depart from it" (Proverbs 22:6).* However, I wonder if any one of us realize that none of us are properly equipped to handle this task. Not only must we teach our children how to live according to God's word, but we must be living examples for them of how to do this. Any time we fail in the teaching or displaying through our lives an accurate portrayal of the truth of God's word, we are failing to 'train up a child in the way he should go'. Besides this, not one of us is saved apart from God's grace, including our children. We cannot impart God's grace to our children, only God can. However, that does not mean we are not responsible for teaching and training our children in the ways of the Lord. Diligent study of God's Word is essential for taking this responsibility seriously, *"You shall love the Lord your*

Lessons in Farm Life

God with all your heart and with all your soul and with all your might. And these words that I command you today shall be on your heart. You shall teach them diligently to your children, and shall talk of them when you sit in your house and when you walk by the way, and when you lie down and when you rise" *(Deuteronomy 6:5-7).* It is imperative to teach our children a love for God, and take every opportunity we can to teach them about God. They need to be aware of the all pervading sense of God's presence, understanding that he sees everything we do, hears everything we say and even knows our every thought. We need to teach our children that the choices and decisions they make should be made with the knowledge that as Christians, (if they are indeed Christians), they are temples of the Holy Spirit, *"Or do you not know that your body is a temple of the Holy Spirit within you, whom you have from God? You are not your own, for you were bought with a price. So glorify God in your body"* *(1 Corinthians 6:19-20).* We were not put on this earth to serve ourselves; we are to be in service to our Lord. **We were bought with a price**; the price being the precious blood of Christ. We need to instill in our children's minds the importance of glorifying God in everything they do. They should look at any kind of act or duty with the view that they are serving God, and so must do so cheerfully and with a proper attitude.

We need to be preparing our children to handle the many responsibilities they will have to bear. It is imperative that we prepare our sons to be the spiritual leaders they need to be within their own homes; to stand

Equipped for the Task

firm in their faith, in order that they may be prepared to teach their own children the importance of obedience to God's commands, and walking in His ways, *"He established a testimony in Jacob and appointed a law in Israel which he commanded our fathers to teach to their children, that the next generation might know them, the children yet unborn, and arise and tell them to their children, so that they should set their hope in God and not forget the works of God, but keep his commandments" (Psalm 78:5-7).* Our sons need to realize the tremendous responsibility that will be theirs as heads of their households. They are ultimately responsible to God to love their wives unconditionally and to teach and train their children in His ways. Notice the verse; **he commanded our fathers** to teach. This does not mean that we, as women, who likely spend more time with our children are exempt from teaching them biblical principles. However, it is the father who must see to it that this teaching is done. He is ultimately responsible to God as the head of the household to oversee the spiritual training of his family.

We also need to teach our sons the importance of handling temptations that may come their way by living lives above reproach. One very important area that we need to do this in is the area of dating, or courtship. Regardless of which method one promotes, if one or the other –or both young people do not have a right relationship with Christ- the method itself will not guarantee a successful marriage. If one's heart is not focused on living for God and his glory, he/she will not be above putting themselves

156

Lessons in Farm Life

in the path of temptation, nor above breaking their marriage vows down the road when things do not go according to their wishes. We need to teach our sons that one's relationship with God must come above all other relationships.

Young men need to be taught how to be proper gentlemen, right from a young boy on up to a young man. They need to be taught to treat a young lady with respect. I like the recommended guidelines of one pastor in the area of courtship. He felt that the physical relationship between a young man and woman who are seeing each other with the intention of marriage should be that of a brother to his sister until they actually do marry. I'm sure some people, maybe even many, would scoff at this, saying that's being a little too prudish. However, it certainly would save a lot of hurt and emotional pain down the road, especially if the couple felt they were not really suited for one another after all. No doubt many pastors and counselors could attest to the varied and multiple problems within a marriage relationship because the couple could not exercise self-control before the honeymoon took place. Any couple who would follow this guideline of total purity within their relationship should be sure to enjoy a far better relationship when they did marry, knowing that each of them had kept themselves pure for their marriage partner. The guideline for total purity within relationships is clearly scriptural, *"Do not rebuke an older man but encourage him as you would a father. **Treat** younger men like brothers,*

Equipped for the Task

older women like mothers, **younger women like sisters, in all purity,"** *(1 Timothy 5:1).*

A good example of a young man who shows us the importance of keeping oneself pure can be found in the story of Jacob's son, the handsome young Joseph. Joseph obviously considered his relationship with God far more important than his relationship with a woman. Joseph, like Daniel, was also a young man taken from the comforts of his own home and exiled in a foreign land. He too, remained firm in his faith, *"The Lord was with Joseph, and he became a successful man, and he was in the house of his Egyptian master"(Genesis 39:2).* Because his master had such confidence in Joseph he left all that he had in Joseph's charge.

We also learn that this handsome young man had captured the eye of his master's wife. Potiphar's wife obviously had no convictions in regard to fidelity within her marriage relationship, for she tempted Joseph to spend time with her that he knew would be wrong for him to do. Joseph did not respond to Potiphar's wife in the way that she had wished for him to. This is the reply he gave to her; *"Behold, because of me my master has no concern about anything in the house and he has put everything that he has in my charge. He is not greater in this house than I am, nor has he kept back anything from me except yourself, because you are his wife. How then can I do this great wickedness and sin against God" (Genesis 39:8-9)?* Joseph rightly acknowledges that his sin would be against God, as all sin is. Unfortunately, other people may experience hurt and pain because of

Lessons in Farm Life

our sin, which should grieve us greatly, but we need to realize that all of our sin is ultimately against our most holy and loving God. When we read on in this story of Joseph and Potiphar's wife, we find that Joseph doesn't just walk away from temptation, he runs, *".. One day, when he went into the house to do his work and none of the men of the house was there in the house, she caught him by his garment, saying, 'Lie with me.' But he left his garment in her hand and fled and got out of the house" (Genesis 39:11-12)*! Oh, to be able to raise our children with such strong convictions against dishonoring God that they would even run from the temptation to sin. We must strive to train our young men to be as diligent in seeking God's guidance each day as Daniel- and as pure in their conduct within their relationships as evidenced in the life of Joseph.

It is also very important that we train our daughters to strive to be godly young women. The more I think about some of the movies that our family has watched over the years, starting with fairy-tale romances, the more I have come to understand the importance of taking time to discuss the content of programs we watch with our children. It is imperative that we teach our children the difference between entertainment and living in the real world. Young children are very impressionable and they can grow up with a wrong idea of relationships in regard to marriage if they are not taught the difference. We need to be instilling in our daughters the importance of living to glorify God, looking out for the needs of others and not making their life's goal to be finding their own prince

159

Equipped for the Task

charming. They should understand it may not even be in God's plan for them to marry. Their most important relationship needs to be with God- above all others. That is the kind of relationship that will bring about a more godly lifestyle. It should be the inner beauty within a young lady that would draw the attention of the kind of man we would want our daughter to marry, (if that is God's will for her) as in the Bible story of Ruth and Boaz.

In the book of Ruth we find another old familiar and favorite story, that of Naomi. I think most of us must know of the story of Naomi, who along with her husband and two sons had moved to Moab due to the famine in their own land. Upon the death of her husband and two sons, one of her daughters-in-law, Ruth, decides to return to the land of Judah with Naomi. Naomi urges Ruth to go back to her people with her sister-in-law Orpah. However, Ruth is adamant in her loyalty to Naomi, *"May the Lord do so to me and more also if anything but death parts me from you" (Ruth 1:17).* So the two go to Judah, and Ruth takes care of Naomi by gleaning in the fields.

Here is a young woman who could have returned to her own people and probably have married again, living comfortably in her own familiar surroundings. However, she chooses to put the needs of her mother-in-law above her own needs and selflessly decides to take care of her. The Lord blesses both Ruth and Naomi by causing her to glean in the field of Boaz, who turns out to be a near relative. Boaz treats Ruth with great kindness and when she questions him as to why he would be so good to one

160

Lessons in Farm Life

who is a stranger to him he replies; *"All that you have done for your mother-in-law since the death of your husband has been fully told to me, and how you left your father and mother and your native land and came to a people that you did not know before. The Lord repay you for what you have done, and a full reward be given you by the Lord, the God of Israel, under whose wings you have taken refuge" (Ruth 2:11-12)!* Boaz also takes note that Ruth does not try to attract the attention of men, *"....you have not gone after young men, whether poor or rich" (Ruth 3:10).* If our young women are taught the importance of putting their relationship to God first, above all others, then when, (or if) the time comes for courting (or dating), they will be far more likely to deal with this very important issue in a way that would glorify their Lord. God first, others needs ahead of our own, and ourselves last of all. Putting things in the proper perspective is most important. Then if they are meant to marry, they will marry a man of God's choosing and not their own, as we see in the case of Ruth. For at the end of Naomi's story, Boaz marries this young woman from Moab, and he and Ruth have a son. And so, Naomi is, of course, overjoyed to be blessed with not only a godly daughter-in-law, but also a godly son-in-law, and to top it off, God blesses her with a beautiful grandson as well. A very happy ending to what started out as a very sad and sober story.

It is so very important that we are properly equipped spiritually to handle every situation within our lives. In a sermon I listened to once, the pastor spoke of the

Equipped for the Task

importance of being in the right spiritual condition ourselves in order to deal with a fellow Christian who has stumbled and is obviously struggling with sin in his life. This may be one of our own children, or a brother or sister in Christ. We may even be aware (or think we are) of sin in the life of someone who is seemingly unaware of it himself. Both of these situations can be very delicate and require one who is strong enough spiritually to be able to handle them.

Thinking on this put me in mind of two stories in the Bible. First of all we will look at the story of David's sin with Bathsheba. We all recognize David as being 'the man after God's own heart', yet he is not immune to the horrendous sin of adultery and, even worse still, the murder of this woman's husband. The story of David's sin with Bathsheba is a familiar one found in the eleventh chapter of second Samuel. When David finds out that his sin has caused Bathsheba to be with child, he has her husband put in the forefront of the battle knowing full well he will be killed, so that he can then be free to take Uriah's wife to be his own. We read on in Chapter 12 that the Lord sent Nathan to David in order to confront him with the seriousness of his sin. Nathan shows great wisdom in his approach to David's sin. Using the analogy of a rich man and a poor man, he caters to David's compassion. The rich man of course, having many flocks and herds, is compared to David with his many wives, and contrasted with the poor man, being Uriah- with just one wife, who had but one little ewe lamb, that he loved and "grew up

162

Lessons in Farm Life

with him and his children', *"It used to eat of his morsel and drink from his cup and lie in his arms, and it was like a daughter to him" (2 Samuel 12:3).* The injustice of the story where this rich man, who had so much and yet, instead of taking from his own abundance, takes the poor man's one little lamb to prepare for a traveler who had come to him, enrages David. His response is; *"As the Lord lives, the man who has done this deserves to die, and he shall restore the lamb fourfold, because he did this thing, and because he had not pity" (2 Samuel 12:5-6).* Then Nathan reveals to David, "You are the man!" David's appropriate response to being confronted with his sin we find in verse thirteen of the same chapter, *"I have sinned against the Lord."*

Nathan could have just come right out and confronted David telling him he had acted very foolishly and should have known better, but he was discerning enough to realize that was not a good approach to take. Nathan was following biblical principles in his dealing with this situation. We are told in Galatians chapter six and verse one that we are to handle these situations gently, *"Brothers, if anyone is caught in any transgression you who are spiritual should restore him in a spirit of gentleness. Keep watch on yourself, lest you too be tempted."* Not only are we to handle these situations with great care and gentleness, but we are also to exercise caution so that we not fall into temptation ourselves, being mindful that even the strongest of Christians are not exempt from falling into great transgression.

163

Equipped for the Task

The fact that we need to be careful to examine our own lives for sin before confronting someone else with theirs, puts me in mind of the story of Job. Here we have a man who had not only been blessed with spiritual blessings, but with great material possessions as well. The Lord allows Satan to bring many disasters into Job's life so that he might be tested. Then after having endured so many tragedies all at once, poor Job suffers from the 'good intentions' of his friends. Eliphaz, Bildad, and Zophar did actually display true signs of sympathy and comfort toward Job; *"They made an appointment together to come to show him sympathy and comfort him.....they raised their voices and wept, ... And they sat with him on the ground seven days and seven nights, and no one spoke a word to him, for they saw that his suffering was very great"* (Job 2:11, 13). However, they might have done better not to have opened their mouths, or to have determined to speak only words of encouragement. Job's comforters' is a familiar phrase, actually used more in sarcasm than anything else. These men evidently lacked the gentleness and compassion through their speech that was needed to bring real comfort to their suffering friend. They thought they were in a spiritual position to deal with Job's circumstance, but they obviously were not. They did not know the reason for Job's suffering, and had they even been right in their implications, they certainly were not handling the situation in an appropriate manner. They were not glorifying God in their approach. In the last chapter of Job we read; *"The Lord said to Eliphaz the Temanite: "My*

Lessons in Farm Life

anger burns against you and against your two friends, for you have not spoken of me what is right, as my servant Job has…." *(Job 42:7).* Then the three men were instructed to make an offering and Job was to pray for them, as God would only accept Job's prayer on their behalf.

It is very important that we go to a person with the right attitude and frame of mind realizing our own weakness to sin. A self- righteous attitude and condemning approach to one's situation will not benefit either side. Matthew 7:1-5 says, *"Judge not, that you be not judged. For with the judgement you pronounce you will be judged, and with the measure you use it will be measured to you. Why do you see the speck that is in your brother's eye, but do not notice the log that is in your own eye? Or how can you say to your brother, Let me take the speck out of your eye, when there is the log in your own eye? You hypocrite, first take the log out of your own eye, and then you will see clearly to take the speck out of your brother's eye."* We are to examine our own lives for sin before attempting to try to help others with theirs. We should never try and correct another person, even our own child, if we are aware of, or in need of, dealing with sin in our own lives. We must repent and deal with our own sin first. In one sermon I listened to on raising children, the pastor made a very chilling remark. He said when our children hear godliness through our mouths yet see wickedness in our lives; we point them to heaven, but lead them to hell, and he repeated his statement to stress his point. This is a very sobering thought, and a very apt reminder to be on our knees before God, seeking His

165

Equipped for the Task

grace and enabling that we not just 'talk the talk', but that we would 'walk the talk' and strive to be faithful role models for our children to follow.

If we truly have our hearts directed toward God, we will be living with an all pervasive sense of His presence, focusing on living our lives to please and serve those around us. We need to be more than just willing to help others out in a practical way, we also need to be aware of, and on the look out for the spiritual needs of those around us. If a brother or sister is in need of encouragement- or if they are stumbling in their walk, we should be there for them, *"Therefore encourage one another and build one another up.." (1 Thessalonians 5:11).*

In neglecting to address matters of concern, in overlooking sin, not wanting to deal with it when we know that we should, we are showing that we are more afraid of offending men than we are of offending God. It is not an easy thing to do, confronting one with sin, for we know the reaction we receive could be very unpleasant. No one likes to be confronted with their sin- or to find themselves in an unpleasant situation. However, in our neglect to confront matters of concern, we are presuming upon God's mercy and goodness, *"So whoever knows the right thing to do and fails to do it, for him it is sin" (James 4:17).* I'm afraid we, as Christians, take sin *far* too lightly. *Matthew 5:4, "Blessed are those who mourn, for they shall be comforted."* The context of this verse would indicate that we need to be mourning over our sin. Our God is a holy

Lessons in Farm Life

God, demanding perfection from His people. We are to be making *every* effort to live holy lives.

We do need to be careful that we not judge the motives or the hearts of those around us, only God can do that. This does not mean that we overlook or turn a blind eye to sin. We most certainly can judge the actions of those around us, *"Do ye not know that the saints shall judge the world? and if the world shall be judged by you, are ye unworthy to judge the smallest matters? Know ye not that we shall judge angels? How much more things that pertain to this life? If then ye have judgements of things pertaining to this life, set them to judge who are least esteemed in the church" (1 Corinthians 6:2-4).* In Romans 15:14 we find this encouragement, *"And I myself am persuaded of you, my brethren, that ye also are full of goodness, filled with all knowledge, able also to admonish one another."* This would indicate that we *are* to be admonishing one another (reproving in a gentle manner). Of course this must be done only by those who are able to practically apply their knowledge of the gospel and it must be done with the right motive, in the spirit of love, and with much prayer, seeking the guidance of the Holy Spirit.

In 1 Corinthians 5:12-13, we find these words; *"For what have I to do with judging outsiders? Is it not those inside the church whom you are to judge? God judges those outside..."* Paul is talking about those within the church who are openly transgressing God's Laws and unrepentant. *"The spiritual person judges all things, but he himself is judged by no man" (1 Corinthians 2:15).* I believe this verse would be

167

Equipped for the Task

referring to a person who is walking in step with the Spirit of God, making *every* effort to live a holy life, one that is above reproach. Again, the admonishing or restoring of others who are dealing with sin in their lives, *must* be done by ones who are in a right relationship with God themselves.

We should also be aware that there are times when one must be strong in their admonition toward another. Jesus dealt very forcefully with the Pharisees of his day because of their hard-hearted hypocrisy, (Matthew 23:15-28). However, He dealt very gently with those who recognized their sin and were ashamed of it, as in the case of the woman at the well, (John 4), and the woman caught in adultery, (John 8:3-11).

Of course we must be aware that we will not handle every situation perfectly. We will stumble and fall ourselves. However, if we are discerning enough to recognize those times and repent of them, then we will be in a much better position to teach others the importance of repentance and godly living within their own lives. We must be living in obedience to God's word and seeking the Spirit's guidance, striving to grow spiritually stronger continually, so that we will be properly equipped for any difficult tasks that lie ahead.

16

Don't Give Up!

Luke 18:1-8

I headed out to the barn this morning in an apprehensive state of mind. I had finally gotten May-belle into a proper routine, or so I thought, where I would give her breakfast, hook her up, get her cleaned off well, and milk until I had nearly filled my one gallon container. I would then let the calf out to nurse, unhook May-belle, leaving them both for a half hour or so, before either coming out myself, or sending my son to turn her out to pasture. Well, all had been going well, until I moved her over into the next pen where my husband had put a new floor down hoping to make things a little easier for me, which it did. It is much nicer to milk on level ground than on the uneven place where I had been milking. For some reason, May-belle started being very ornery after being moved over here. She didn't like me cleaning her off and

Don't Give Up!

she would lift her foot over and over and even kick at me as I attempted to do so. I did get some milk, but in order to even get half of what I usually do, I had to milk with one hand in order to keep her foot still with the other. Needless to say I was getting rather frustrated. Then, to make matters worse, she realized she had more freedom in this pen to move around. So, even with being hooked, she could move her bulk clear over so that she was standing under the window and against the wall, where I could not reach the side I needed to milk. She may not be a big cow, but she is still a lot stronger than I am and throwing her stubbornness into the mix, makes the situation most unpleasant. As she stood there under the window looking at me as if to say, "I'm not moving until you let my baby in here." I had several things go through my mind. No, I wasn't cussing, though had this happened to me a few years ago, I likely would have been.

I must admit, I felt my eyes start to prick suspiciously as there were tears threatening to flow. I was so disappointed. I had thought that I had her all trained and wouldn't have any more trouble with my morning milking. Then I pondered the situation, and thought to myself, you are being tested here, how are you going to handle it? If this had happened a few years ago, as I already indicated, I likely would have been doing some cussing. In fact I probably would have been doing more than cussing, I'd have been kicking and slapping as well. I would have been crying, wailing, and wondering how she could do this to me, after I had her all set into a routine. The tears would

170

Lessons in Farm Life

be streaming down my face in exasperation. I would be out of breath from pushing, shoving and exerting my best efforts to try and get this stubborn bossy to do what I wanted her to do. She should know how it goes by now, it really isn't that difficult. She knows I will let her baby out as soon as I get my gallon of milk. This once 'well mannered and cooperative' cow should not be giving me all this grief. Then I would have finally let the calf out with these thoughts in mind; "I can't do this, I don't want to do this, I don't have time for this. It's just too much trouble and bother." Essentially my thought would have been, "I give up!"

But for some reason I did not do any of those things. And this is why; it it is because God has put the music to the lyrics that I have known for so long. I feel as if I am living my life in step with God's Holy Spirit. I realized I was being tested and it was for a purpose. I then determined that I would not give up, I was not going to give in to May-belle. I was not going to give in to the devil's temptation for me to lose my temper, causing me to sin. I was going to do what I knew needed to be done and that was to get the rest of my milk before letting May-belle's calf out to nurse. She was not going to have her way just because she was being stubborn and disagreeable. So, I unhooked her, shut her in the pen and went back up to the house to have breakfast and devotions with my husband and son before my husband had to go off to work. I then went back out to the barn taking more feed with me. This time I also took a couple of long boards as

171

Don't Give Up!

well, nailing them up as a temporary means of keeping her away from her window spot. Then I tossed some more feed into her bin, cleaned her a bit more and proceeded to use both hands this time to finish my milking. I was most thankful and relieved that she was a lot more cooperative now. So, I got my milk, let the calf out, unhooked May, and headed back to the house, singing as I went. I was also praising God for the work of His Holy Spirit in my life, the victory over my sin, and the inspiration for this story. The lesson here I hope will be easy to determine; and that lesson is; "Don't give up!"

This was not a major trial to undergo but God *can* keep us calm and even give us a song in our hearts during the major upheavals of our lives as well, as indicated here in the following two passages of scripture; *"Now when Herod was about to bring him out, on that very night,* **Peter was sleeping between two soldiers***, bound with two chains"* *(Acts 12:6).* Can you imagine? How in the world could he be calm enough to sleep being chained to a soldier on either side? This is the kind of peace and calm that could only come from trusting in an Almighty God who is able to save. And God does save Peter from his predicament; for, as we read on in the chapter, God sends an angel to free Peter from his chains and bring him out of the prison, *"When Peter came to himself, he said, "Now I am sure that the Lord has sent his angel and rescued me from the hands of Herod and from all that the Jewish people were expecting"* *(Acts 12:11).*

Lessons in Farm Life

Later on we come across a couple of fellows who are enjoying a sing- song while they are imprisoned in the city of Philippi, *"About midnight Paul and Silas were singing hymns to God, and the prisoners were listening to them" (Acts 16:25).* They were not singing because they were happy to be in prison. We do not rejoice in the terrible, sometimes heart-wrenching circumstances we may have to go through. We are certainly not happy when this happens. However, we do rejoice in the God who is working through those circumstances for our good and His glory. Reading on we find how God sent an earthquake to open the prison doors and as a result, the jailer, realizing that he will lose his life if he loses his prisoners, determines to put an end to it himself. In answer to Paul's cry, assuring him they were all still there, the jailer rushes in to the prison; *"...trembling with fear he fell down before Paul and Silas. Then he brought them out and said, 'Sirs, what must I do to be saved?'" (Acts 16: 29–30).* This is an important lesson to learn- that God will give us a song, even in the midst of trying circumstances, when we faithfully trust Him to work through those circumstances for our good. How many of us would sing if we were locked up in a prison cell? Not many I'm sure. Yet, because of the faithful testimony Paul and Silas demonstrated throughout that unpleasant situation, we read on in the chapter that the Philippian jailer (the very man who was responsible to see that they remained in the prison) and his family are converted. God used Paul and Silas' dreadful circumstances for His glory and their good, *"And he* (the jailer) *took them the same hour*

173

Don't Give Up!

of the night and washed their wounds; and he was baptized at once, he and all his family. Then he brought them to his house and set food before them. And he rejoiced along with his entire household that he had believed in God," (Acts 16:33-34) What an amazing God we serve.

So many things come to mind in thinking on the statement of not giving up; First of all I think of our children and the stress and frustrations we encounter in the rearing of them. At times, when they give us many headaches and a lot of stress and frustration, how often do we think to ourselves, "This is just too hard; I don't want the hassle. It takes too much out of me. I don't have time for this. I give up!" Then we give in to whatever demands our children are making in order to save the time, trouble, and bother of dealing with a difficult situation.

When they are very young and naughty, perhaps they may make a scene in the grocery store because they want something. How often do we just give in to them in order to save the hassle and embarrassment of dealing with a loud and unruly child with watching eyes all around us? Then when they get a little older and demand certain rights and privileges, even if we know granting those rights to them would not be in their best interests, we give in, because it just is too frustrating and time consuming to try and get them to see things our way. So many times, in order to save the unpleasantness of a confrontation, we simply give in, again and again... If our children are not taught at a very young age to honor and obey, certain situations within their lives, and ours, will become even

Lessons in Farm Life

more difficult as they grow older. Then, we should not be surprised, as when these same children as young adults, do not treat us as their parents, with the respect and honor the bible commands them to, (Ephesians 6:1-2).

The teaching, training and instilling of godly values in the lives of our children must be a priority starting when they are very young. Discipline also must be administered in a loving and consistent way until they are prepared to make wise decisions on their own; if not, we had better be prepared for major struggles and heartache as they grow older. Thankfully, we can take comfort in knowing that even if we are experiencing struggles and trials within our families for whatever reason, that God knows what we are dealing with and we can go to Him in prayer, and He will answer that prayer. We can also take comfort in knowing that when we turn to our Heavenly Father in repentance due to our own neglect of this teaching in the lives of *our* children that He will forgive us and enable us to be the faithful role model that we should have been earlier on, so that we can be a help and encouragement to them in the godly training of their own children.

I'm sure Augustine's mother, Monica, must have grown weary and frustrated as she spent not just days, weeks or even months, but many years in fervent prayer for her wayward son. Augustine had cast off his faith in Christ as a young man and turned to heresies and a life of immorality. For nearly nine years he was caught in the cultic practices of the Manichaeans, a religious sect from Persia. His desperate mother begged a bishop to speak

Don't Give Up!

to her son and reveal to him the error of his ways. The bishop, being wary of competition with Augustine, (who had a great and well-known reputation as an orator), told her that a mind as subtle and acute as that of her son could not continue long in such deceptive reasoning, and he would not even attempt to speak with him. However Monica continued her attempts to persuade him with much pleading and many tears. Finally, the bishop, who had become annoyed by her persistence, yet moved by her tears, answered her roughly with a mingling of compassion and kindness, "Go, go! Leave me alone. Live on as you are living. It is not possible that the son of such tears should be lost." This persistent mother prayed for *seventeen years* for the conversion of her son.

Praise God, there did indeed come a day when this faithful mother's prayers were answered, as her son began his journey home. Augustine was guided to Rome and then farther north where, after listening to the most eminent churchman of that day, Saint Ambrose, he left the Manichaean cult and began to study the Christian faith once again. Then, as we know, Augustine was converted to faith in Christ and went on to fulfil all of his mother's hopes, living out the answer to her many prayers. How she must have rejoiced that day when he came and told her of his conversion. How she must have praised God. How thankful she must have been for the burden God gave her to persist in her prayers for her son.

May we follow in this Christian mother's example, faithfully and fervently praying for any and all those for

Lessons in Farm Life

whom He has given us a burden for. No matter what the circumstance, regardless of the hopelessness of the situation, just pray, and keep on praying, remembering that our God has the victory over all of sin. He is sovereign and in complete control over our lives and the lives of our loved ones as well and we can leave them in His most competent and providential care.

I know my husband is thankful that he did not give up on me, as I am myself. At the point in time where God started to reveal the areas in my life that were not right, I sent a letter to our pastor outlining what I saw as the problem areas of my life and asking him to pray for me and for our family. I would like to tell you that it was at that point where things really started turning around for the better, but I must be honest and admit that certain circumstances within our lives became much worse. Unfortunately, more often than not, it takes a lot of hard knocks to bring us to our senses. Sometimes the Lord brings us to the end of ourselves. He allows us to hit rock bottom in order to bring us to the point where we finally acknowledge our helplessness. He shows us our need to cry out to our God in repentance, realizing that we need the help that only He can give and that it is only through Him that we can ever hope to attain any kind of an effective Christian testimony in this fallen world.

It was a little over one year later that I sent a second letter to our pastor. This time the letter that I sent was filled with praise for the work of grace that God had been doing in my life. Here is a quote from a portion of this

Don't Give Up!

second letter that I gave to our pastor. I hope this insert will encourage any who may be going through a difficult and seemingly hopeless time with a loved one.

"It has taken a lot of hard lessons to learn and much pain as God has revealed to me so many areas in my life that needed to change. My poor husband was frustrated time and again as he tried to point out some of the problems I had. His attempts were not successful as I did not receive his admonishments well. Finally he was at the point of giving up– then he started to pray– pray for our marriage, (for me) that God would do a work in my heart– and by His grace and mercy He did. He removed that dark cloud of gloom and brought the 'Son' into my life. He has filled my heart with such joy and a peace in knowing that He is in complete control and I can trust all of our lives fully to His providential care. ...God has truly been so good to us. He has done so much for us and we are so undeserving. I pray we continue to grow in the knowledge and love of our great God and Savior and that He would empower us to share that love with others. I am filled with gratitude and praise for His mercy and grace."

If you are married and living with a spouse that is bitter and discontented, Don't give up! Continue in prayer for that loved one, love her/him, and leave them in God's hands.

If you are living with a wife who is difficult and controlling, who will not recognize the importance of submission to the headship of her husband, "Don't give up on her!" Pray for her consistently, love her, and leave her in God's hands.

178

Lessons in Farm Life

If you are living with an unfaithful spouse, one who is an unbeliever or one who is disobedient, rebelling against God's commands; Don't give up on him/her! Pray for that loved one continually, take advantage of opportunities to point your spouse to Christ, love him/her, and leave that loved one in God's hands.

If your home is being torn apart due to the waywardness and rebellion of your teenage son or daughter, Never give up on him or her. Pray for wisdom and discernment in knowing how to deal with difficult situations. Pray for and love him/her, and leave that loved one in God's hands.

No matter what the situation, whether God has laid upon your heart the burden to pray for a child, spouse, friend, sibling, pastor or even an acquaintance; regardless of the circumstance, even if it appears to be hopeless, remember that our God is in control. He knows all about it, and if that loved one belongs to God, He is working out His purpose and plan to bring him/her into a right relationship with Him. Even if those circumstances aren't to our liking; even if they are heart-wrenching and full of pain, we can trust that He is working through all things for the good of those who love him.

In thinking of the importance of persistence, the parable of the widow and the unrighteous judge comes to mind. Jesus told this parable to encourage us not to give up, *"And He told them a parable to the effect that they ought always to pray and not lose heart. He said, 'In a*

Don't Give Up!

certain city there was a judge who neither feared God nor respected man. And there was a widow in that city, who kept coming to him and saying, Give me justice against my adversary. For a while he refused, but afterward he said to himself, 'Though I neither fear God nor respect man, yet because this widow keeps bothering me, I will give her justice, so that she will not beat me down by her continual coming.' And the Lord said, Hear what the unrighteous judge says. And will not God give justice to his elect, who cry to him day and night? Will he delay long over them? I tell you, he will give justice to them speedily'" (Luke 18:1-8).*

Another comforting passage is found in Joel 2:25-26, *"I will restore to you the years that the swarming locust has eaten, the hopper, the destroyer, and the cutter, my great army, which I sent among you. You shall eat in plenty and be satisfied, and praise the name of the Lord your God, who has dealt wondrously with you."* Though we cannot go back and make any changes in the past, we can hold on to the promises of God's word today and tomorrow and for as long as He gives us here on this earth, and determine by His grace to live from this day on for His honor and glory and not to fulfill our own selfish desires.

Here is a portion of David's prayer of repentance after Nathan had come to him rebuking him for his sin with Bathsheba, *"Create in me a clean heart O God, and renew a right spirit within me. Cast me not away from your presence, and take not your Holy Spirit from me. Restore to me the joy of your salvation" (Psalm 51:10-12).* We can be assured that God will grant the petitions we ask of Him

Lessons in Farm Life

when we know they are according to His will. If He has promised, He will do it. Let us have the confidence of Abraham, who did not waver concerning the promise of God, *"But he grew strong in his faith as he gave glory to God, fully convinced that God was able to do what he had promised" (Romans 4:20-21).* We must have faith to believe that God will do what He has promised us according to His word, *"And without faith it is impossible to please him, for whoever would draw near to God must believe that he exists and that he rewards those who seek him" (Hebrews 11:6).* This little phrase, "Whoever would draw near to God," is certainly a clear indication that we are responsible to be diligently seeking our God through the study of his word and prayer.

We are in need of one another's prayers. If a brother or sister in Christ comes to us with *any* kind of concern we need to take it seriously and display to that 'loved one' a true compassion and love by taking that matter to prayer before God. It seems as if there is far too little emphasis placed on prayer and the effects of it. A well-known pastor has said, "In some mysterious way beyond our understanding, God requires intercessory prayer as a necessary wheel in the machinery of His providence. He commits to people the responsibility of moving this wheel". A very clear indication of the importance for us to have a full realization of man's responsibility, *our* responsibility as God's people. The Bible tells us to be constant in prayer, (Romans 12:12). It tells us not to be anxious about anything, but to take

181

Don't Give Up!

it all to God in prayer, (Philippians 4:6). The Scriptures tell us to continue steadfastly in prayer, (Colossians 4:2). And in James 5:16, we are told to; *"..confess your sins to one another and pray for one another, that you may be healed. The prayer of a righteous person has great power as it is working."*

We *must* be fighting for our families, and we need to be looking to each other in support of this. It is a battle we are in, a spiritual battle, and we need to be helping each other fight this battle, for the devil *is* going about like a roaring lion, seeking whom he may devour *(Ephesians 6:10-12).*

While this is God's promise to us as His people, we need take note that these verses are in future tense, *"I will cleanse you. And I will give you a new heart, and a new spirit I will put within you. And I will remove the heart of stone from your flesh and give you a heart of flesh. And I will put my Spirit within you, and cause you to walk in my statutes and be careful to obey my rules"* *(Ezekiel 36:25-27).* He will do this! At Christ's second coming and when we are fully glorified, we, and our loved ones who are in Christ, will no longer struggle with sin. God *will* cause us to walk in his ways and perfectly obey Him. However, as long as we live on this earth with this sin nature, we must understand that we will continue to struggle with sin. Our responsibility is to be drawing near to our God, praying persistently and waiting patiently for Him to answer our prayers. We should never give up in our prayers for our loved

Lessons in Farm Life

ones or for any of those God lays upon our hearts to pray for. He will be far more merciful to us as a loving Heavenly Father when we persist in our prayers than the unrighteous judge was in the account of the persistent widow. Just remember; Don't give up!

17

To Be..
Or Not to Be..

Matthew 10:37-38

Some years ago our daughter acquired a kitten. We had been without a cat for awhile and living on a hobby farm, with lots of grain around, we really needed a cat to help keep the mice population under control. This kitten was coal black and really quite cute, as most kittens are. The people who gave us this kitten assured us that it was male in gender. I had made it very clear that I did not want a female kitten. Female kittens grow up to be cats that have more, more, and more kittens. Since I did not wish to be enveloped by more and more cats, I decided a male kitten would be more preferrable. So, we brought this 'male' kitten home, and our daughter named him Mowgli.

Lessons in Farm Life

This cute little kitten grew over the months and naturally became a cat. One day I noticed something rather odd concerning our daughter's cat. He was out in the barnyard and I saw another cat there with him. This other cat was one of our neighbor's tom cats. Knowing how toms tend to fight with one another, I was hoping they wouldn't didn't get into a scrap. Well, my fears were unfounded as I realized they were anything but fighting. To my amazement and consternation, this is when I found out that our daughter's cat was, in fact, not of male gender after all. We had not seen the need to bother checking for ourselves to find out whether this kitten was definitely a male at the time we brought it home, as the people we received it from had actually been informed by a vet of its gender. I was not too stunned as to be inactive in giving out a holler and chasing our neighbor's cat from the barnyard. In order to deter any further male attentions, we did not waste too much time in making an appointment at the vet for 'Mowgli,' whom we continued to refer to as 'he' for some weeks to follow.

Thinking back on the 'Mowgli mix-up' made me ponder on the fact that we, as 'professing Christians' may even prove to be totally different from the claim that we profess. The reason I started pondering over this incident is because there have been so many times that I have thought back to years gone by and been made aware of how very different a person I am now from what I was even three years ago. Not that I would seem to be a lot different to most people who have known me

185

To Be.. Or Not to Be..

over the years, though I would hope they have seen some differences in me in recent years. However, if you were to question my husband, who, having lived with me all these years, and knowing me better than anyone, (next to God, of course), I know he would attest to the fact that I am a different person from what I was earlier on in our marriage. The reason for this difference is because of the working of God's Holy Spirit in my life. In all honesty, I would have to admit that I wasn't truly 'converted' for a good many of the years I claimed to be a Christian. I was not actually 'saved' from my sins, for I was still enslaved by them. Discontentment, bitterness, resentment were all prevalent within my life and the sin of self-absorption actually enslaved me. How could I truly call myself a Christian when I failed to show a love for God in the way that I lived? I didn't really have a desire to study God's word as I should have, which is one indication of a love for God. I truly didn't have the kind of love for his people that I should have had, nor the desire to serve others as I have in more recent years. I would do things for people, but I'm ashamed to admit that a lot of times, I was motivated more out of an obligation to do so, rather than out of a love for God and for others. I was too self-absorbed to be of much use for the sake of the gospel. I was, in fact, still in bondage to my sin. I thank God that He has truly set me free from that bondage.

Something that I heard in a recent sermon really got me thinking. The pastor said that one can have a change in lifestyle without ever having a change of heart.

186

Lessons in Farm Life

In other words, we can make a profession of faith, live a very religious lifestyle and yet not really experience a true conversion within our hearts. That is a very sobering thought; it made me question how many people within our churches, claiming to be Christians, in fact, are not truly converted after all? How many pastors even, may be standing in the pulpit each Sabbath day preaching God's word and proclaiming his grace and mercy to others, yet not truly experienced it for themselves?

In the book of Acts we find an excellent example of one who had been truly converted by the grace and mercy of our Great God and Savior. Before Saul's conversion, he was a persecutor of the church of Christ, *"Saul, still breathing threats and murder against the disciples of the Lord, went to the high priest and asked him for letters to the synagogues at Damascus, so that if he found any belonging to the Way, men or women, he might bring them bound to Jerusalem" (Acts 9:1-3)*. Reading on in verses 3-9, we find the account of Saul's dramatic conversion and how God sends one of His disciples, by the name of Ananias to Saul, in order to lay hands on him so he may regain his sight. At first Ananias is hesitant to go to Saul, knowing full well of this man's reputation, *"Lord, I have heard from many about this man, how much evil he has done to your saints at Jerusalem" (Acts 9: 13).* God assures Ananias that He has made Saul a 'chosen instrument' to carry His name to the Gentiles. We read on down to verse 19 and find that Saul was with the disciples at Damascus for some days, *"And immediately he proclaimed Jesus in the synagogues, saying, 'He*

To Be.. Or Not to Be..

is the Son of God.'" And all who heard him were amazed and said, *"Is not this the man who made havoc in Jerusalem of those who called upon this name?"* Here we have Saul himself speaking; *"I have become all things to all people, that by all means I might save some. I do all for the sake of the gospel" (1 Corinthians 9:22-23).*

This man, Saul, who once could not do enough to be rid of God's people, became a man who could not do enough to win people to God. Here we have Saul, also called Paul speaking again; *"For to me to live is Christ, and to die is gain" (Philippians 1:21).* That is what it means to be a true convert of Jesus Christ; to be so focused on living for Him that we *know* that to be with Him would be even better than living on this earth at all. Though we may not be called to be preachers as Paul was, we still must show through the living out of our daily lives that we are not what we once were. If we are truly in Christ our whole focus is changed. We should be able to say with Paul, 'For to me to live is Christ, and to die is gain.' If we are not ready to die and be with Christ, we are not prepared to really live for Him.

Paul was most definitely a new creation. His old life was past, along with its old practices. The Bible tells us if we are in Christ, that we are a new creation, *"Therefore, if anyone is in Christ, he is a new creation. The old has passed away; behold, the new has come" (2 Corinthians 5:17).* We will be totally different 'in Christ', *"We know that our old self was crucified with him in order that the body of sin might be brought to nothing, so that we would no longer be enslaved*

188

Lessons in Farm Life

to sin...Let not sin therefore reign in your mortal bodies, to make you obey its passions" (Romans 6:6, 12). Christ died for our sins, in order that we might be freed from the bondage of them. Therefore, if sin still has a stronghold within our lives as ones who profess Christ, we are dealing with a major problem. We need to be on our knees, in confession and repentance. We also need to be mindful to spend time each day in God's word and in prayer to our Heavenly Father.

Another clear illustration of how we show that we are true Christians is by the love and concern that we show to others, regardless of the circumstances that we ourselves, may be in. In Genesis, we find the account of Joseph, another devout man of God. In one of our earlier stories, we read of how Joseph had been tempted by Potiphar's wife. Due to this incident, and her lie to her husband about what really happened with Joseph, he was unjustly thrown into prison. Now, the human response to such an unjust action would be to whine and complain and do some major protesting. However, we do not find this to be Joseph's response. In fact, because of Joseph's exemplary behavior, the keeper of the prison puts him in charge of all the other prisoners, *"The Lord was with Joseph and showed him steadfast love and gave him favor in the sight of the keeper of the prison" (Genesis 39: 21).*

In chapter 40, we can read that some time after Joseph's imprisonment, two officers of the King, the baker and cup bearer, are put into the prison where Joseph is confined. That night they each experienced disturbing dreams. The

To Be.. Or Not to Be..

next morning their troubled countenance prompts Joseph to respond to them in the following manner; *"When Joseph came to them in the morning, he saw that they were troubled. So he asked Pharaoh's officers… 'Why are your faces downcast today" (Genesis 40: 6-7)?* If we really think about this situation, would we not be surprised at Joseph's behavior? Here is a man who has been put into prison for a crime he did not commit. He has been there for some time and yet he notices the despondent behavior of two other men in the prison with him. He not only notices their behavior, he shows his concern by enquiring about it. Joseph could have been pretty despondent himself, having his own little pity party, but he wasn't. Why not? He wasn't feeling sorry for himself because, as one whose desire was to honor God in his relationships, he was looking out for the needs of others around him. His focus was on God and others as ours also should be. By showing his concern for their unhappiness, he opens up an opportunity to be a witness to them. If we are too caught up in our own little world, lost in our self-absorption, we won't have time to look out for the needs of those around us. We will miss out on so many opportunities, not only to be a blessing to those around us, but also to be blessed by God, through the many opportunities to serve that He is bound to bring our way when we put our focus on Him.

Let us be mindful of the parable of the rich ruler, who must have lived a fairly good and moral lifestyle, for he claimed to have kept the commandments from his youth, yet when faced with the decision to choose between

Lessons in Farm Life

following Christ and enjoying his earthly possessions, the true condition of his heart becomes exposed. This man was concerned to have an assurance of eternal life. However, when Jesus told him that he lacked one thing necessary to secure this assurance, he went away very sad, for he was extremely rich, *"One thing you still lack, sell all that you have and distribute to the poor, and you will have treasure in heaven; and come, follow me" (Luke 18: 22).* When Jesus challenged the rich ruler to give up all his possessions, it became apparent that he did not really understand the commandments at all; for when he was faced with the choice to follow Christ or to enjoy all the world had to offer him; it was clear that his earthly possessions were of more importance to him than God was. The Bible tells us that we should not place a higher value on anyone or anything than the value we place on our relationship to God, *"Whoever loves father or mother more than me is not worthy of me, and whoever loves son or daughter more than me is not worthy of me. And whoever does not take his cross and follow me is not worthy of me" (Matthew 10: 37-38).* We must be willing to give our all for the sake of the kingdom.

I wonder if we were placed in the rich ruler's position, to choose between God and worldly pleasures and possessions, what this would show to those around us about the state of our hearts? Would we show that earthly possessions and worldly comforts are more important to us than our relationship to God? Are those comforts more important to us than knowing that our children

191

To Be.. Or Not to Be..

are prepared for eternity? Would we far rather store up treasures on this earth to enjoy for a brief span of time, than to store up treasures in heaven to enjoy for ever?

We need to ask ourselves, Are we true followers of Christ, ones who display a real love for the things of the Lord and a desire to serve others, or not? Or are we just 'professing Christians', appearing to be righteous on the surface, yet actually hiding our true identity, which, if uncovered, would prove that it is not truly in Christ? We can be like so many out there who live a good moral lifestyle, hoping it will be good enough to merit our way into heaven, or we can enjoy a real relationship with the One who has accomplished all that was required to inherit eternal life on our behalf. 'To be.. or *not* to be..?' *that* is the question. What will *our* answer be?

18

Pursuing Presumptions

Psalm 19:13

Well, we are off with the old and on to the new here, once again, in regards to the dog that now resides with us here on the Weston Farm. Not too long after our daughter's marriage, she came and took Tia, her German Shepherd to live with her and her new husband. I wasn't too sorry to see Tia go, though she was a very quiet and gentle dog. However, she was also big, and we had to keep a very close eye on her when she came in heat, which proved to be rather inconvenient at times.

Anyway, the Lord opened up an opportunity for us to get another dog, and this lovely little dog is very close to the breed that we have said we would always like to own. The dog we now have actually looks like a miniature

Pursuing Presumptions

Lassie. I couldn't believe it when my husband brought him home. He had come across this advertisement on the internet from a lady wanting a good home for her dog, so he called her. As it turned out, he was the first one to call, so he and our son went to see him. When they arrived, the little fellow; Shiloh, by name, actually took to my husband right away, which amazed the little dog's owner. She told me later on, when she came to visit, that no one had been able to get near him, except for her, not even her friend, unless she was toting treats. Confiding her belief that the dog had been abused before she got him, she expressed her surprise that he would let my husband come right up to him. As a result, she had been quite pleased for my husband to take Shiloh home. This lady, who had never met us before in her life, just gave us this beautiful dog along with a bag of dog food and leashes. I couldn't believe it. She said she felt guilty for keeping him, as she worked so many hours and the little fellow was alone too much. I knew that ultimately, it was God that brought this beautiful dog into our lives- through the compassion of Shiloh's owner, and that was no presumption. Through the outworking of God's providence in bringing Shiloh into our lives, this section on presumption has been brought to my mind as a result. I have no doubt another good reason for Shiloh becoming a part of our family is to teach us more lessons we are in need of learning, for they have started already.

When we first brought 'Shiloh' home, he was <u>so</u> good. We never once heard him bark for the first couple of

Lessons in Farm Life

days and I thought, 'Oh, great. he's going to be a nice quiet dog.' Well, after a few days, he found his voice. He wasn't yappy; just barked once in a while. I could handle that. And then, after a little more time went by, when people came in, he would bark- and bark- and bark! It was actually becoming rather annoying, this barking when people came in. Well, we'd just have to train him out of it, I said. We have been working with him some, not as much as we should though. Watching "The Dog Whisperer" has been helpful in providing the information we need to teach him to be calmer and more submissive, because he also has a bad habit of jumping up on us when we go to take him outside. Our son especially gets rather perturbed, since Shiloh's toenails are rather sharp and as a result of his jumping up he received quite a painful scratch from them one day.

Actually, I don't really have a tie up to this story, because it isn't finished yet. We still have more training to do with 'Shiloh, before he can become the calm submissive, well-mannered dog we would like him to be. However, there is still a very good lesson to be learned here. That lesson is; **Never Presume**. I had presumed that Shiloh would be a nice, quiet, well-mannered dog after he had first been brought home, however, first impressions can be deceiving. Now, my hope is that he *will become* a quiet and well-mannered dog after we spend some major time working with him-however, I should not presume this will be the case. Only time will tell for sure.

197

Pursuing Presumptions

Now, I want to talk about presumptions in relation to our Christian walk. We, as Christians need to be so *very* careful not to get led into the sin of presumption. It really is a terrible sin if we stop and think about it. After being inspired with the idea for this story, I asked my husband if he could give me a good illustration from the Bible that would demonstrate the seriousness of this sin. He pointed me to the story of Joshua and Caleb and the other spies sent to search out the land of Canaan. If you are not familiar with that story, it is found in Numbers chapter 13. God had told Moses to send men to spy out the land of Canaan. At the end of forty days, these men returned to give their report. The report was that the land was a bountiful land, flowing with milk and honey. However, they also reported the fact that the people dwelling in the land were strong and very large. Among these spies were two men by the names of Joshua and Caleb. These men were like David, in that they had complete confidence in their God to give them the victory over their enemies. Here we find Caleb speaking; *"Let us go up at once and occupy it, for we are well able to overcome it" (Numbers 13:30).* However, the majority of the spies said; *"We are not able to go up against the people, for they are stronger than we are. So they brought to the people of Israel a bad report of the land that they had spied out, saying, 'The land, through which we have gone to spy it out, is a land that devours its inhabitants, and all the people that we saw in it are of great height. And there we saw the Nephilim (the sons of Anak, who come from*

Lessons in Farm Life

the Nephilim), and we seemed to ourselves like grasshoppers, and so we seemed to them'" (Numbers 13:32-22).

This story reminds me so much of David and Goliath. David stood all alone against Goliath, the only one who had complete trust and confidence in God's ability to deliver him. Here we have Joshua and Caleb, along with Moses and Aaron, standing alone, the only ones there among the people of God, who, like David, had complete trust and confidence in their Almighty God to deliver them. This analogy made me wonder- actually it made me realize- how very few Davids there are, how very few men like Joshua and Caleb. It made me wonder how many of us, who call ourselves Christians, are willing to stand against the odds, even if we find ourselves all alone as David did.

God tells us in John 15:1-6 that He is the vine and we are the branches. He also tells us that He takes away any branches that do not bear fruit, and he prunes any that do bear, so that they may bear even more fruit. (Of course, the pruning process is compared to the many struggles and trials of the Christian life.) The branch cannot bear any fruit unless it abides in the vine, so we cannot bear any fruit unless we abide in Christ, by reading and listening to his word, and spending time in prayer. We must be diligent in exposing ourselves to those things that will draw us into a closer walk with our Lord. If we have no desire to do this, and therefore do not display any signs of fruit in our lives- we are showing ourselves to be branches that are not fruit bearing and will be taken away.

Pursuing Presumptions

Returning to the story of Joshua and Caleb, we find the people weeping and grumbling against Moses and Aaron. They were even discussing the possibility of choosing a new leader and going back to Egypt. Can you imagine? They would choose to go back into slavery, rather than to trust in their God to save them. This was the same God who had brought them out of that slavery in the first place. Then we have Moses, Aaron, Joshua and Caleb all encouraging the people to trust in God and imploring them not to rebel against the Lord, *"If the Lord delight in us, he will bring us into this land and give it to us, a land that flows with milk and honey. Only do not rebel against the Lord. And do not fear the people of the land, for they are bread for us. Their protection is removed from them, and the Lord is with us; do not fear them" (Numbers 14:8-9).* What do these men, (who encouraged God's people to trust in their Almighty God, the One who made himself known to them through so many miracles and delivered them from their bondage) get for their faithfulness to their Lord? We find out in verse 10, *"Then all the congregation said to stone them with stones."* It doesn't seem quite right does it? Unfortunately, people are the same today as they were back then in the time of Joshua's day. It is still the people (who claim to know God) within the church who are the most offensive and likely to cause division. This is sad, but true. When we fail to follow God's commands, we display to those outside the church a distortion of the gospel, (Galatians 5:16-25). The problems unbelievers hear of within the church and the lack of commitment they see

200

Lessons in Farm Life

in 'professing Christians' confirms to them- they have no need of Christ. Either they do not see the people inside the church as being much different from themselves, or they see them as being worse. The sad fact is, some of us who claim to be Christian, are really not. We may be what is known as a nominal Christian, meaning in name only; one who has an intellectual understanding, but not a heart knowledge. These 'professing Christians' have no real desire to change the way they live, for they are too comfortable as they are. They have no desire to really take up their cross and follow Christ, *"Whoever does not bear his own cross and come after me cannot be my disciple (Luke 14:27).*

Going back to Joshua and Caleb; As a result of the people's rebellion, they were prevented from being able to enter the Promised Land, *"Not one shall come into the land where I swore that I would make you dwell, except Caleb the son of Jephunneh and Joshua the son of Nun" (Numbers 14:30).* We also find that the spies themselves who brought the bad report, *"...died by plague before the Lord. Of those men who went to spy out the land, only Joshua... and Caleb... remained alive" (Numbers 14:37-38).*

After Moses tells the people what happened as a result of the bad report these spies brought, they 'mourned greatly'. *"And they rose early in the morning and went up to the heights of the hill country, saying, 'Here we are. We will go up to the place that the Lord has promised, for we have sinned..' But Moses said, 'Why now are you transgressing the command of the Lord, when that will not succeed? Do not go up, for the*

201

Pursuing Presumptions

*Lord is not among you, lest you be struck down before your enemies. For there the Amalekites and the Canaanites are facing you, and you shall fall by the sword. Because you have turned back from following the Lord, the Lord will not be with you.' But they **presumed** to go up to the heights of the hill country, although neither the ark of the covenant of the Lord nor Moses departed out of the camp. Then the Amalekites and the Canaanites who lived in that hill country came down and defeated them and pursued them, even to Hormah" (Numbers 14:40–45).*

Isn't that so much like us today as ones who call ourselves Christians? We *presume* the Lord is with us, and we go out to fight our enemies (the forces of darkness in spiritual battles,) when He, in fact, may *not be* with us at all. He will not be with us *if* we are not abiding in Him; if we are not making use of the instructions He has given us whereby we can know Him and serve him in a way that would honor and bring Him glory. We must not go out into the world each day without the protection of our armour. See Ephesians 6:10-18. We must not fool ourselves, thinking just because we go to church, are baptized, and perhaps even church members, that God is with us. We must not presume that we are doing everything right, when in fact we may not be. So many people who call themselves Christians are living with just a head knowledge of what Christianity is all about. I was one of those 'professing Christians', right up until approximately 2 1/2 years ago. I wish I could explain the tremendous difference it makes in ones' life. I know if you

Lessons in Farm Life

ask my family, they can tell you, I am different. I'm not the same wife and mother I was just over two years ago. I also know that, if you ask my family, they will tell you the change that has come over me is a change for the better. Oh, so much better. We need to be so very careful not to be living with the sin of presumption. We need to pray as David did; *"keep back your servant also from presumptuous sins; let them not have dominion over me! Then I shall be blameless and innocent of great transgression" (Psalm 19:13).*

Up until two weeks ago, I myself, had been living with the burden of a terrible 'sin of presumption'. I had actually been living with *this* sin of presumption for well over a year. Even during the past two weeks I have caught myself making presumptions, time and again (just to discover that I am constantly making wrong presumptions); this sin is one that is so easy to get caught up in. I haven't made the kind of presumption that says God is with me, when He really isn't, for I know He has been with me this past year. The way He has led and guided me is proof of that, especially in these past two weeks that we have gone through. No, this presumption that I had made was due to something my husband and I found out about over a year ago that involved a close member of our family. Because this loved one was not willing to talk about it, I made presumptions that I should not have made. I made these presumptions based on a few things that I did have knowledge of; One being the present day circumstances of this loved one, and another being certain circumstances that occurred many years ago involving several people that

203

Pursuing Presumptions

were well known to me in my younger years. However, we must be so very careful not to make presumptions based on a few facts here and there that we do have knowledge of. If we do not have all of the facts surrounding a matter, we should not make presumptions that actually could, and often times will, turn out to be false.

There were many times when I would agonize over this situation that we were so much in the dark about. I would make presumptions, and my husband would warn me against doing so. He warned me because he knew the importance of thinking more highly of others, *"Do nothing out of selfish ambition or vain conceit, but in humility consider others better than yourselves. Each of you should look not only to your own interests, but also to the interests of others" (Philippians 2:3-4).* This next passage is another clear indication that we are to be careful of how we think of others; *"Finally, brothers, whatever is true, whatever is noble, whatever is right, whatever is pure, whatever is lovely, whatever is admirable- if anything is excellent or praiseworthy- think about such things" (Philippians 4:8).* In other words if we are tempted to think of another with a critical or condemning spirit- we are sinning. If we slander another person's character, by saying things we do not even know to be true, or speak unkindly of him/her by bringing up negative character traits in a disparaging way, we are disobeying our Lord's command, for this is clearly against the teaching in scripture. And yet, I would be so tempted to be critical and condemning, and I did give in to that temptation many times, knowing about

204

Lessons in Farm Life

the struggles and hard times others had gone through in similar circumstances. I would think to myself, this loved one's behaviour is so similar to another that I had known who had endured much trauma. Then I would start presuming again, thinking whatever happened must have been dreadful. I struggled so much with forgiveness throughout this period of time, forgiveness toward one who I presumed had had such a dreadful influence over this loved one's life. Yet, I did not realize that I was the one who needed to be forgiven- forgiven for harboring a critical and condemning spirit. We can only act upon the basis of what we know to be true at a given time, and even had I known whatever act committed against this close family member was as horrid as I suspected, I still had no right to be condemning, or unkind, for to do so would not be praiseworthy. We must recall our Lord's instructions and remember the kindness and mercy He has displayed to us in our sin, and even though we may not think of our own sin as deserving of condemnation- it is. Our pride and condemning attitude is just as deserving of God's judgement as any transgression of God's Law. We must recall Jesus' words in the fifth chapter of Matthew; *"You have heard that it was said to the people long ago, Do not murder, and anyone who murders will be subject to judgement. But I tell you that anyone who is angry with his brother will be subject to judgement. ...You have heard that it was said, Do not commit adultery. But I tell you that anyone who looks at a woman lustfully has already committed adultery with her in his heart" (Matthew 5:21-22, 27-28).*

Pursuing Presumptions

Jesus is showing the people their lack of understanding the true fulfillment of the law here, helping us to see that anger and hatred toward another is just as much a sin as murder; in the same way that lust is as much a sin as adultery or any other sexually immoral act. I should clarify here that we cannot think to ourselves- we may as well go out and commit adultery if we have lust in our hearts.. certainly not. That would be a far more grievous sin, that would bring greater judgement on ourselves and also cause others to suffer great pain through the consequences of it. The point being made here is that anything short of God's perfection is sin, and as Christians- God calls us to a very high standard. We are to strive after holiness- and so we must put to death any kind of temptation to sin that would lead us to will-fully transgress the Law of God, (See Colossians 3:5-10).

We need also to be careful in the way we respond to a personal offence- for we can behave as if a transgression committed against us or one of our loved ones is the worst sin ever. We need to ask ourselves; Are we in the place of God? We need to remember that all sin is against our holy God, and be mindful that we are not to condemn the actions of others with a harsh, critical, or unforgiving spirit. If one displays actions that are in no way Christlike, we are called to treat that person as one in need of Christ- with love, mercy and if need be- forgiveness.

We must be very careful not to give in to feelings of anger or bitterness toward any who may have influenced one of our loved ones toward leading an ungodly

Lessons in Farm Life

lifestyle. We need to remember that when giving in to these emotions (that would indicate a heart lacking in forgiveness), we are sinning- breaking God's commands, *"O Lord, who shall sojourn in your tent? Who shall dwell on your holy hill? He who walks blamelessly and does what is right and speaks truth in his heart ; who does not slander with his tongue and does no evil to his neighbor, nor takes up a reproach against his friend;" (Psalm 15:1-3).* When we show signs of bitterness and anger in our hearts, we are not being blameless. When we speak ill of someone, we are not resisting the temptation to gossip or slander. When we confront a friend or family member with any other motivation outside of love, we are being a stumbling block and leaving the way open for further sin and transgression of God's Law.

Although a loved one may have been severely influenced by another toward making choices and decisions that would not be for his or her good; we do need to understand that whoever may have had that influence over them would not be guilty for their present day choices and decisions. We all must take the responsibility for our present day transgressions despite the negative influences that we may have been surrounded by in our past. We must remember that sin comes from within. It is not the outside influences that cause us to sin- they certainly do effect us, tempting us to give in to the sinful desires that are in our hearts. However, we will not give in to those temptations if the desire for that sin is not within our heart to start with. We are responsible for our own actions

207

Pursuing Presumptions

despite the negative influences, we have been, or are even now, surrounded by, *"There is nothing outside a person that by going into him can defile him, but the things that come out of a person are what defile him.... For from within, out of the heart of man, come evil thoughts, sexual immorality, theft, murder, adultery, coveting, wickedness, deceit, sensuality, envy, slander, pride, foolishness. All these evil things come from within, and they defile a person" (Mark 7:15, 21-23).* We should take note that envy, slander, and pride are all listed in the same sentence with adultery, murder, and sexual immorality. They are all deserving of God's judgement, not one of them is any more acceptable than another. If we find any of these traits within our lives as Christians, we must repent of them and seek God's forgiveness- for we are sinning.

If we are a 'professing Christian', and yet choose not to live according to God's clear instructions within his word, we are giving in to the sin that lies within us and transgressing God's Laws and we will suffer the consequences of our poor choices. Those consequences may have severe and long lasting repercussions; *"But each person is tempted when he is lured and enticed by his own desire. Then desire when it has conceived gives birth to sin, and sin when it is fully grown brings forth death" (James 1:14-15).*

When traumatic events occur- such as a close member of the family leaving their spouse or the spouse of that family member leaving him/her, it can be devastating for the rest of the family. That wandering family member may be struggling in their faith. Perhaps they have allowed

208

Lessons in Farm Life

themselves to become too busy each day to take time to spend in the word or in prayer (or perhaps they are in genuine need of conversion). It is imperative that we surround ourselves with good and godly influences so our relationship with the Lord will not grow cold. When we allow ungodly influences into our marriage, we can be sure it will have a negative effect and we will suffer the consequences. If we find ourselves constantly lured in the wrong direction, and failing to seek after God, we should be questioning whether or not we are truly in Christ; because without Christ, we have no way of choosing to do good, *"None is righteous, no, not one; no one understands; no one seeks for God. All have turned aside; together they have become worthless; no one does good, not even one" (Romans 3:11-12).*

We need also understand that even if we do surround ourselves with good influences- and yet are not seeking Christ's enabling grace- we will just end up living moral, acceptable according to the world, kind of lives- just like the Pharisees. We must understand God's standard for us is holiness, *"Strive for peace with everyone, and for the holiness without which no one will see the Lord" (Hebrews 12:14).* In Matthew 5:48, we are told, *"You therefore must be perfect, as your heavenly Father is perfect."* If we do not have a hatred for our sin and the desire for perfection, we will not be striving after holiness. If our desire is not to draw near to God, this will become apparent, not only in the kind of company we choose to keep, but also in the kind of thoughts we think, and it will eventually become

209

Pursuing Presumptions

apparent in our actions as well. We must ask ourselves; Is it our desire to please and honor Christ- to actually take captive every thought in obedience to Him? Is our chief goal in life to glorify God?

If this is not our desire, we may be showing ourselves to be one of many, who call themselves Christians, yet, have not experienced a real heart knowledge of what life *can* be like when one is filled with the Holy Spirit and living with a desire to truly honor and glorify their Lord. These people may call themselves Christian, but they are carnal, for they continue to expose themselves to ungodly influences, being sucked in by them. They listen to all the voices that deceive them into thinking they can find happiness here, there, or anywhere, but in Christ alone.

I, myself was such a person. I was essentially living a lie, presuming myself to be a very devoted and sincere Christian, when in fact, I was not. God exposed to me the wickedness of my heart. I look back now and shudder at the stumbling block I must have been. My children grew up with both parents professing to be Christians. I know they wouldn't have had a problem with my husband's profession. However, I have no doubt they would have seen a lot of discrepancies in my life. I can remember different times, during those troublesome teen years (which really didn't need to be so troublesome) just wanting to know so much- where the desires of my children's hearts lay- and I didn't even know for certain where my own were. I had such a log in my own eye, that, sadly, I couldn't see

Lessons in Farm Life

clearly to help my own children with the branch that was in theirs.

I am so thankful that we are blessed with this wonderful promise in the following verses of John 15:7-8; *"If you abide in me, and my words in you, ask whatever you wish, and it will be done for you. By this my Father is glorified, that you bear much fruit and so prove to be my disciples."* I have been claiming this promise for *so* long. I have reminded God of it many times over these past couple of years as I have been striving to draw near to God. For over a year now, my husband and I have turned on the <u>Truth for Life</u> series. I don't know if there has been even one day that we haven't listened to some of Alistair Begg's sermons. I believe I have grown more in the past year, than I had in the previous thirty years. I have also determined to spend time on my knees every day in prayer. I know there have been very few days that I was unable to do this. And I am confident that God will answer the prayer of my heart.

As I draw near to him, I can feel him drawing near to me; *"Draw near to God, and he will draw near to you"* (James 4:8). He has definitely drawn near to me, most especially these past two weeks. It has been as if He has been right by my side, guiding me and giving me the strength to get through each day. The strength He has given, has been beyond human capabilities as I have been going through each day on anywhere from one to three or four hours of sleep the previous night. I do want to make clear the reason for my sleeplessness is not due to worry. Most nights it has been because my husband and I have

Pursuing Presumptions

been up discussing scripture and praying. I actually had one night, the one I slept the least, that I just couldn't get a song out of my head. It just kept going over and over in my mind; the one, "Isn't He Wonderful? Wonderful, Wonderful, Isn't Jesus my Lord, wonderful? Eyes have seen, ears have heard, it's recorded in God's Word, isn't Jesus my Lord, wonderful?" It truly is amazing, not only the peace and calm that He can give us in the midst of trials, but the joy as well. I can be joyful because I am trusting in my Lord and striving to be obedient to His Word; *"Rejoice in the Lord always; again I say rejoice" (Philippians 4:4).* I know He will give me his peace as I pray and trust in Him; *"do not be anxious about anything, but in prayer and supplication with thanksgiving let your requests be made known to God. And the peace of God, which surpasses all understanding, will guard your hearts and your minds in Christ Jesus" (Philippians 4:6-7).* Our God never lies, He will be faithful to fulfil his promises. I can assure you that we can trust fully in His most wholly wise and providential care. Praise God, and pray to God that He keep us from the sin of presumption.

19

Fickle, Fleeting, Or.. Forever!

Proverbs 17:17

I am carrying on here with my story of Shiloh, for the Lord has shown me another good lesson that can be learned from our experiences with this little dog. Remember how I said when he first came that I couldn't believe this lady had given us this beautiful dog? Well, on first sight I believed he was beautiful. I was so thrilled that we had been given such a handsome looking animal and for the first few days he had been so quiet that I just couldn't believe we would be given such a perfect pet. Then, after a week or so, I realized he wasn't quite the perfect pet I had thought him to be. Then, when the newness had worn off, the responsibility of owning another dog set in, along with the realization that this

Fickle, Fleeting, Or.. Forever!

dog was going to take a lot more work than some of our other dogs. He not only had the bad habit of jumping up, he also started a bad habit of taking off whenever we were all indoors. As a result, we had to either bring him inside with us or chain him up outside, unless we were with him. This worked fine for awhile, until he started leaving even when one of us was outside with him. I must admit I was thinking maybe this beautiful dog was not such a fantastic gift after all. In fact, when my husband accidentally ran over a dog belonging to one of our neighbours, and felt so very dreadful, I wouldn't have been too sorry if he had offered this little dog to her to as he suggested. However, when we took into consideration the fact that the dog's owner was an elderly lady, plus the knowledge that our dog had some bad habits, we decided our newest canine would not be a suitable replacement.

I got musing over how fickle my feelings have been toward this little fellow. When he first came I was so thrilled that this beautiful little dog, who looked like a miniature version of Lassie, was just given to us. I made so much of him for the first little while, until the newness wore off and the bad habits started surfacing. He wasn't quite so endearing to me when he didn't turn out to be the way I had hoped he would. I wanted an animal that I didn't need to put any time into, one that would just be exactly what I wanted it to be without the need for me to put forth any effort in the process. I would pet him and make much of him as long as he was behaving the way I wanted him to, but when he stepped out of line and

214

Lessons in Farm Life

started to show some of those annoying habits, I would distance myself from him, even half wishing he hadn't been brought here to begin with. Then I got thinking, we haven't even had Shiloh for three months, and here I am, almost wishing we hadn't gotten him to begin with.

I have really been feeling ashamed of my feelings toward this cute little canine. The more I muse over these circumstances, the more I realize that if we want Shiloh to be a well-mannered dog, one who can be useful to us on the farm, then we are going to have to put more effort into our relationship with him. We can't expect him to be obedient and submissive to an owner who really doesn't want to put the time into training him to be obedient and submissive. He is just a young dog and he needs for us to demonstrate our care for him and our willingness to put the time into training him to be the dog we would have him to be.

As I mused over my unjust feelings toward this poor little mite, the similarity between my situation here with Shiloh and the way we, ourselves, treat other people, even those we call friends, really struck me with a blow.

How many times do we strike up new relationships, including friendships with other Christians only to have the relationship dissipate over time because of our fickle feelings toward them? It's so new and exciting at first, meeting other people, new people who come to our church or those we meet in other places where we have interests in common. We strike up a friendship, which may become a close relationship, that may even last for many

Fickle, Fleeting, Or.. Forever!

years, until with time, comes change. This may be due to circumstances changing in their lives, or in ours. Then one or the other starts to see things they don't really care for in their 'friend', whether it be their methods of child-rearing, their lack of tactfulness in certain areas, or perhaps there has even been an unresolved misunderstanding, (the sin of presumption creeps in). Regardless of the issue this friend has... for certain reasons, one or the other- or both start to distance themselves from each other, until what was once a very close and thriving friendship has become... a non-existent relationship.

We need to look to our Lord for the kind of example that friends *should* be to one another, especially if we are ones who profess to know Christ. I am so very thankful that our Lord is not fickle and changeable like us. We can count on him to be there for us no matter what. He is always loyal, always faithful, never misunderstanding... one who sticks closer than a brother, *"A man of many companions may come to ruin, but there is a friend who sticks closer than a brother" (Proverbs 18:24).*

As always we can look to the Word to find examples of those who have followed in our Lord's footsteps- and, of course, those who haven't. A very good example of true friendship can be found in the relationship between David and Jonathan. Here we have the son of a king, one who is heir to the throne, befriending a shepherd boy who is a servant of his father. This is not just a casual acquaintance, nor a fleeting friendship. This is the kind of friendship that lasts a lifetime, through good times and

Lessons in Farm Life

bad. We are told in *1 Samuel 18:3-4; "Then Jonathan made a covenant with David, because he loved him as his own soul. And Jonathan stripped himself of the robe that was on him and gave it to David, and his armour and even his sword and his bow and his belt."* Jonathan's gifts to David display not only his loyalty, but also his willingness that David, as God's chosen one, should succeed to the throne. We see this more clearly on in chapter 23 when Saul is seeking to destroy David's life, and Jonathan comes to encourage his friend; *"Do not fear, for the hand of Saul my father shall not find you. You shall be king over Israel, and I shall be next to you. Saul my father also knows this" (1 Samuel 23:17).* There is no hint of jealousy or resentment in this young man's tone. How many of us could so easily step back to let another take a desired position within our own lives? As we are taught in God's word, we must be able to deny ourselves; and that is not an easy thing to do.

We come across the covenant that Jonathan and David made with each other when we find Jonathan speaking; *"...do not cut off your steadfast love from my house forever, when the Lord cuts off every one of the enemies of David from the face of the earth... And Jonathan made a covenant with the house of David... and Jonathan made David swear again by his love for him, for he loved him as his own soul" (1 Samuel 20:14-17).*

When David hears news of the deaths of Saul and Jonathan, he laments their passing and remembers the great love that Jonathan had for him, *"Saul and Jonathan, beloved and lovely! In life and in death they were not divided; ....I am*

Fickle, Fleeting, Or.. Forever!

distressed for you, my brother Jonathan; very pleasant have you been to me; your love to me was extraordinary, surpassing the love of women" (2 Samuel 1: 23, 26).

Some time after David had been crowned king he asks if there is anyone left of Saul's household to whom he might show kindness for his friend, Jonathan's, sake. When he found out that Jonathan had a son still living, David sends for him. Now, being the only one left of the royal family, Mephibosheth, Jonathan's son, is more than a little nervous to be summoned by the king, and rightly so, considering the fact that many times, the reigning king could and would, get rid of any competitor to the throne. However, Jonathan's crippled son did not need to fear any such action on the part of this true friend of his father's. When Mephibosheth is summoned to David's presence, this is the response he receives from him; *"Do not fear, for I will show you kindness for the sake of your father Jonathan, and I will restore to you all the land of Saul your father, and you shall eat at my table always" (2 Samuel 9:7). "And Mephibosheth had a young son, whose name was Mica. And all who lived in Ziba's house became Mephibosheth's servants. So Mephibosheth lived in Jerusalem, for he ate always at the king's table" (2 Samuel 9:12-13).* This is surely a good example of a true friendship, for it lasted not only throughout the years of David's relationship with Jonathan, but it extended far beyond that, through the relationship he established with Jonathan's son, Mephibosheth, for the sake of the friend that he had loved so dearly. Wouldn't we all love to have

Lessons in Farm Life

a friend like David? Shouldn't we all strive to *be* a friend like David?

As we read on in 2 Samuel we find not only another example of true friendship, as seen in Hushai, a loyal friend to David, but also an example of a betrayal of friendship in Ahithophel. These examples are discovered at the time David is found fleeing from his son Absalom, who had conspired against his father in hopes of attaining the throne. Ahithophel, who once was a valued counselor of David, had betrayed his friendship and gone over to side with Absalom. When David hears of Ahithophel's conspiracy he is found praying; *"O Lord, please turn the counsel of Ahithophel into foolishness" (2 Samuel 15:31).* No sooner had David uttered this prayer than God provided the answer, in the form of a man called Hushai. Hushai had come to meet David with his coat torn and dirt upon his head, signifying his grief and sorrow at what has taken place. David tells Hushai; *"...if you return to the city and say to Absalom, I will be your servant, O king, as I have been your father's servant in time past, so now I will be your servant, then you will defeat for me the counsel of Ahithophel.... So, Hushai, David's friend, came into the city, just as Absalom was entering Jerusalem" (2 Samuel 15: 34, 37).*

Then we can read on in the sixteenth and seventeenth chapters of 2 Samuel, how Hushai, *"David's friend,"* does indeed defeat the good counsel of Ahithophel, *"And Absalom and all the men of Israel said, 'The counsel of Hushai the Archite is better than the counsel of Ahithophel.' For the Lord had ordained to defeat the good counsel of Ahithophel,*

Fickle, Fleeting, Or.. Forever!

so that the Lord might bring harm upon Absalom" (2 Samuel 17:14). Hushai then sent word to David about his counsel in order to warn him, and in so doing saved his life and the lives of his men. When Ahithophel realized his counsel had been rejected, he set his house in order and hanged himself- a shameful end to the life of a betraying friend. It is too bad that he had not remained loyal to God's chosen one, as David's true friend, Hushai, had done.

I have also been impressed with how this comparison of our feelings toward our 'friends' can be used within the marriage relationship. I am speaking again of normal case scenarios here; two people claiming to be Christians, who have been happily married to one another. In the first few weeks, months, or even years of our marriage, we may be quite enamoured with one another. However, after the 'honeymoon' is over and we get to *really* know one another, we may find our spouse not to be exactly the way we thought he or she would be in certain situations. He may not be the spiritual leader we anticipated or perhaps he is not as strict (or too strict) a disciplinarian with the children... She may not be the kind of housekeeper we expected, or maybe she is a terrible cook, etc... The reason we may be discontent with our spouse is irrelevant. In the exchange of vows between the couple, the pastor does not ask each one if they *feel* they *could* stay married to the other for a lifetime. He asks each of them "*will you*" make this commitment, or "*do you*" vow before God to be committed to one another. The vow is not based on *feeling*, it is based on *will*- making a commitment to one another

220

Lessons in Farm Life

regardless of circumstances, *"It is a snare to say rashly, It is holy, and to reflect only after making vows," (Proverbs 20:25).* In other words, we should not even consider entering a marriage covenant unless we have seriously considered the commitment we are vowing to take *beforehand.* The fact of the matter is- both parties make a vow before God and man to stay committed to each other, "for better or worse, in sickness and in health, for richer or poor, *till death due us part."* In Numbers, we find Moses urging the people not to make rash vows; *"This is what the Lord has commanded. If a man vows a vow to the Lord, or swears an oath to bind himself by a pledge, he shall not break his word. He shall do according to all that proceeds out of his mouth"* (Numbers 30:1-2). In Ecclesiastes, Solomon also stresses the importance of keeping one's vows, *"When you vow a vow to God, do not delay paying it, for he has no pleasure in fools. Pay what you vow.* **It is better that you should not vow than that you should vow and not pay.** *Let not your mouth lead you into sin, and do not say before the messenger that it was a mistake. Why should God be angry at your voice and destroy the work of your hands? For when dreams increase and words grow many, there is vanity, but God is the one you must fear"* (Ecclesiastes 5:4-7).

Unfortunately even those who profess to know Christ show their lack of fear of God by their actions in regards to their marriage vows. We must continue to pray for God's work of grace in the lives of any of our loved ones who may fall into this same category. When one makes a decision to break their marriage vow, that decision to leave his/her

221

Fickle, Fleeting, Or.. Forever!

spouse is a clear indication of their rebellion against God. (Again, I am speaking of normal case scenarios here, not cases where abuse may be in effect). In running from the commitment of a marriage vow- one shows evidence that he/she is running from God. When we do not accept and follow God's rules for our role within the marriage relationship, we are arguing with God, telling Him we do not think His ways are the best. Yet, if we would even attempt to follow His standards for a husband and a wife; we would most certainly find that they are far better than our own. Sadly, more times than not, we decide to follow our own ways, which are the world's ways, and are always centered on self and not on God.

Within the world's eyes, if you come to decide your spouse is not to your liking, you can simply get a divorce and 'try again'. Unfortunately, 'professing Christians' are also falling into this trap. How often do we hear of 'Christian' marriages ending, even after several years of living together? When this happens, we are succumbing to the world's way of thinking, disregarding the seriousness of the vows we have taken before God; trying to excuse our behaviour because of the failure of our spouse to meet our needs. Thinking we deserve better, we decide to bail out of our marriage to try and find someone else who *will* meet our needs. There is one thing we must realize - we will *never* find someone who will meet all of our needs and desires. We cannot meet the spiritual needs of our spouse- only God can. We must also realize that one of the purposes of marriage is to conform us to the image of

Lessons in Farm Life

Christ. Putting two sinners together with the purpose of displaying the gospel to the world through their marriage and family lifestyle is one of the many ways God uses to sanctify His people. It can be a very effective means, if we are doing our part- by seeking Him and striving to obey His commands.

I'm afraid many of us have failed terribly to fulfil the roles required of us in scripture. Either the husband is not understanding his role to love his wife unconditionally and sacrificially or the wife is not understanding or accepting her role to submit to the headship of her husband. It may be that neither one of us is attempting to fulfil the role God has given as outlined within His Word. If only we would understand and realize how much better life- and marriage can be if we would only seek to follow God's guidelines as husbands and wives.

If we happen to be in the category of those who have not outwardly broken our marriage vows, we need to be careful not to be looking down our noses at those who have. In entering into the covenant of marriage, we each took vows before God- and even if we have not outwardly broken those vows, we may not actually be keeping them inwardly in the way that we should. I think of Jesus' sermon on the mount in this, and his teaching that to lust after another is to commit adultery in one's heart. If, as husbands or wives, we are not remaining true to our spouse in *every* way- we are not fulfilling our vows.

If we are not striving to keep God's commands in regard to our roles as husband and wife as outlined in

Fickle, Fleeting, Or.. Forever!

scripture- we are failing to keep those vows. We need to understand if we fail to show love to our spouse for whatever reason, we are neglecting to honor the vow we took to love our spouse- for better or worse. True love is not a selfish love. It is a love where we strive to put the needs of the other ahead of our own. I'm afraid there may be many times each of us fails to keep our marriage vows in the way that we should. When we fail to obey God's greatest command; to love God with all our heart and to love our neighbour (or spouse) as ourselves, we are not fulfilling those vows. If we each, as ones who claim to be followers of Christ would love God as we should, and put the needs of others over our own, then we should not be suffering any 'major' problems within the relationships we have with one another- especially within our marriage.

We *are* sinners, so our marriages will not be perfect; but if we are truly striving to fulfil the roles God has given us as outlined in scripture- our marriage should be the most harmonious of all of our relationships. Our spouse should be our *best* friend, next to Christ, of course- for as two who have been joined together, we are now one, *"Therefore a man shall leave his father and his mother and hold fast to his wife, and they shall become one flesh" (Genesis 2:24).*

Yet, how many times might we speak of our 'friend' or 'spouse' to others in an uncomplimentary manner? Oh, sometimes we may use the excuse, "I just want to tell you this so you can pray for this situation..." Perhaps we may be looking for sympathy from a friend, by relating some of the downfalls of our spouse, *"A dishonest man spreads strife,*

Lessons in Farm Life

and a whisperer separates close friends" (Proverbs 16:28). In other words, this is someone who is talking behind another person's back; gossiping. More times than not, the thing that destroys a relationship, is sinful gossip, which is relating bad news behind someone's back from impure motives, or even slandering someone's character. When we are trying to decide whether or not we should relate information about someone else, we should ask ourselves these questions: What is my motivation for wanting to pass on this information? Is it truly honorable, or is it at all questionable? Is the information I am about to relate truly accurate?

Sometimes we must confront a friend with the intention of admonishing them for something we see that is not God honoring in his/her life. Before we do this, we must be careful to ask ourselves if we are going to that friend in the right spirit- humbly realizing our own weakness to sin; *"Brothers, if anyone is caught in any transgression, you who are spiritual should restore him in a spirit of gentleness. Keep watch on yourself, lest you too be tempted"*, (Galatians 6:1).

The Bible tells us; *"Faithful are the wounds of a friend; profuse are the kisses of an enemy"* (Proverbs 27:6). In other words, you should be able to trust the wounds, or rebuke of a friend, but you cannot trust the flattery of an enemy. If a friend wounds, it is for our good, intended to help us, as was in the case of Nathan when he rebuked David for his sin with Bathsheba (2 Samuel 12). However, we must

Fickle, Fleeting, Or.. Forever!

exercise caution when receiving compliments from one who is not truly a friend.

Proverbs 17:17 tells us that; *"A friend loves at all times,"* In other words, a friend is a friend no matter what; he/she will be there through thick and through thin, good times and bad. None of this 'fair weather' friendship: the kind of friend who is one that will only stick with you as long as you measure up to his/her standards, as long as everything runs along smoothly, but as soon as there comes a bump in the road, an offence of any kind, off they go in the opposite direction. A true friend is one who will be loyal, giving and *for*giving.

The Bible talks very clearly on how forgiving we ought to be; *"Then Peter came up and said to him, Lord, how often will my brother sin against me, and I forgive him? As many as seven times? Jesus said to him, I do not say to you seven times, but seventy times seven" (Matthew 18:21).* In other words, we are to forgive as many times as we are asked. Does this mean we must know there is true repentance? If someone has come to us several times over asking forgiveness for the same offense, we would likely doubt their sincerity, would we not? Yet, Jesus says to forgive continually, not just two or three or seven times, but over and over and over until you lose count. We are not to judge if one is showing a godly repentance, we are to be obedient to God's command to exercise forgiveness an untold number of times. God alone is in the position to judge another person's heart. We are only able to judge actions. And if

Lessons in Farm Life

someone comes with an apology and asks forgiveness, we are to accept that apology and forgive the offense.

When we read on in Matthew 18, we find the parable of the unforgiving servant. It really puts things into perspective when we are considering this issue of forgiveness. If we would stop and consider just how great a debt our Heavenly Father forgave us; and the price Christ paid for our sins, how can we *not* be willing to forgive the offenses against us, when they truly are minor in comparison. I am not meaning to downplay some of the cruel and horrendous acts committed toward people, but when we stop and consider those acts will affect us for a brief period of time- while we live on this earth. Can we truly afford to be unforgiving, knowing how it will affect us for all of eternity, *"For if you forgive others their trespasses, your heavenly father will forgive you, but if you do not forgive others their trespasses, neither will your Father forgive your trespasses" (Matthew 6:14-15)?* If our trespasses (sins) are unforgiven, that would indicate that we are not truly children of God, and therefore subject to the wrath of God and punishment of our sins. See Matthew 18:34-35.

A true friend will be willing to forgive any offense, no matter how grievous. A true friend is one ... like Jesus, *"Greater love hath no man than this, that someone lay down his life for his friends" (John 15:13).* Our Lord has shown us the ultimate friendship in his self-sacrificing love, as he died on the cross on our behalf. He lay down his life for us while we were still in our sin, *"For one will scarcely die for a righteous person- though perhaps for a good person one would*

Fickle, Fleeting, Or.. Forever!

dare even to die– but God shows his love for us in that while we were still sinners, Christ died for us" (Romans 5:7-8). Jesus tells us we are his friends *if* we follow his commands, *"You are my friends if you do what I command you" (John 15:14).*

A true test of our friendship with Christ is our obedience to Him. Abraham shows a very good example of one who was willing to obey Christ, no matter what. He willingly pulled up stakes and moved his family from their native home to follow God's commands. This man, who has been called 'the friend of God' also willingly takes the son of his old age, Isaac, the one God had promised to make of him a great nation, and lays him on an altar, fully intending to sacrifice him at God's command. He was willing to do whatever God commanded him. Are we willing to do the same? Although we know we will never be called to literally sacrifice our sons or daughters on an altar, we may be called to sacrifice them in other ways. Many of those circumstances may not be to our liking, but we must trust that God knows what He is doing. One way we may be called on to sacrifice our children is to commit them to God's care in the field of their careers– which may mean they would have to move to a distant country or province. We must be willing for them to follow God's leading even if it means we may not be as close to them as we would like to be. May we be the kind of friend that Abraham was in our obedience to God.

How 'true' a friendship do we really have with those we call our friends? Is it fleeting or forever? How true a friendship do we have with our Lord? Are we willing to

228

Lessons in Farm Life

give him our all, in obedience to his commands? Let us be the kind of friend that is forever; never fickle, never fleeting, but faithful and true, showing the only real example of a 'forever friend' through our Lord and Savior, Jesus Christ.

20

Showing His Sovereignty

Isaiah 46:9-11

I have been enjoying watching this series of DVDs called, <u>Dog Whisperer</u> with Cesar Millan. Some of the situations he has to deal with are actually quite amusing. If you haven't heard of him, he is an expert at handling dogs with behavioural problems. It is really quite amazing to watch how he handles all the various problems these owners deal with in their dogs. Some of them are even at the point of feeling they need to put their dogs down due to bad biting habits. Many of them come across his advertisement and as a result give him a call, in hopes of-what to them would be a miracle that will prevent them from having to put down a beloved pet.

Lessons in Farm Life

Of course there is nothing miraculous about the way this man deals with the behavioural problems of these pets. It is due more to the knowledge he has obtained as a result of working with dogs for so many years. It is really amusing to watch how some of these dogs actually 'rule the roost.' Regardless of how big or small some of these dogs are, they are practically sovereign in their domain. *They* are the ones controlling their owner's actions, by their bad behavior, rather than the other way around. One little girl had a huge Rottweiler, and one evening we watched as *he* took *her* for a walk. Another dog would not let its owner near in order to trim his fur, and it was just a little squirt of a thing, but vicious when the owner attempted to 'step over the line'.

We have been watching these shows, as I indicated in a previous section, in order to help us put a stop to some of the bad habits Shiloh has. He is doing some better, as we are trying to be more consistent in taking him for walks and making sure he knows *who* is the boss- letting him know he is not sovereign over *this* domain. Actually we would like to be able to train him to herd our cows. It would be great if he could put them in when they happen to get out. I had actually been thinking we might be getting to the end of our hobby farming. However, Dolly, the cow I had hoped to send for hamburger as she hadn't calved in the Spring, is looking very much as if she is going to have a calf late this Fall. Also, both of our other cows that did calve had heifers, and to top it off, my husband intends to follow up on an e-mail from

231

Showing His Sovereignty

a fellow with Highland bulls for sale. So, I'm thinking-we're going to be hobby farming for a few more years to come. I had actually been at the point of just wanting to be rid of the animals. I had been wishing for an easier life with the freedom to come and go. However, I really don't mind keeping them longer now. In fact, I'm starting to like the smell of the barn again. It really is amazing how God can change one's perspective on life.

Getting back to the dog whisperer, Cesar says over and over it is most important for your dog to know that you are the dominant leader. A dog follows someone who is dominant, not submissive. The dog has to be taught that he/she is to be the submissive one and the owner is to let the dog know that he/she is the dominant leader. That is the only way an owner/dog relationship can be what it should be, which is peaceable and free of major conflict between the two. If they are each carrying out their respective roles, this will result in a more harmonious relationship between dog and owner.

This is the same way it should be in our relationship with God. We don't have to worry about God carrying out His role. He is sovereign Lord over all. We are His people and our role is to be submissive in our relationship to our sovereign God. However, when we, by our rebellious behavior attempt to take control, and go our own way, this will only lead to conflict and disharmony in our relationship with God.

The point of this section is as the title says; <u>Showing His Sovereignty.</u> Our God is sovereign over all things

Lessons in Farm Life

and all people and we will understand this clearly when we live according to His teaching. However, when we fail to live in accordance to His Word, He will still show His sovereignty, through His judgment of those who are not His children and through his correction of those who are. Those who belong in God's family must understand the importance of being obedient to His commands.

Just as Shiloh is helpless to correct his behavioural problems without our help, so are we, helpless to correct our sin problems without God's help. God, as our Master, also teaches and trains us in the way He wants us to behave. He does this through His word and by the help of His Holy Spirit, (2 Timothy 3:16, 17). That is why it is so very important that we are reading and studying his word, and seeking the enabling of the Spirit to help us live holy lives, *"..the Holy Spirit, whom the Father will send in my name, ..will teach you all things.."* (John 14:26). *"For the grace of God that brings salvation...teaches us to say 'No' to ungodliness and worldly passions, and to live self-controlled, upright and godly lives in this present age"* (Titus 2:11-12).

Unfortunately, there are members of our family who have strayed from seeking God through His word, and the lives those loved ones now live are evident to this sad fact. We continue to pray fervently for God to do a mighty work of grace in the life of our family. It certainly hasn't been very smooth sailing these past few weeks. In fact I took a very bad fall in my faith just the other night. Up until that time, I had myself convinced that circumstances really weren't so bad, but then I found out they were far worse

233

Showing His Sovereignty

than I could have ever imagined. I was in great distress. I didn't lose my cool, or burst into tears, but I did get angry. I was angry with God because I believed he would protect our loved ones from certain ungodly influences. After all, I had been offering up a specific prayer in regard to this knowing of one of the weaknesses of a close relation. I just couldn't believe that God would let this happen. I was so discouraged, I had been so confident that He was going to fix everything, and to do it quickly. I wanted all of our family to be together for Thanksgiving. I cried out to Him in anger and frustration. "You promised!" I wailed. And I've been claiming that promise for *so* long. I know it must be your will for certain circumstances within our family to be made right. It must be, for through it you would be glorified. Why aren't you doing it? And after having so much praise in my heart all week, thinking all the heartache would soon be over, I lost it. I couldn't hear the music, and the praise was missing from my heart. I was downcast and despondent.

And then, praise God for this strong man of faith he gave me for a husband. God reminded me through him, that our ways are not God's ways, and we are told to wait upon the Lord, *"but they who wait for the Lord shall renew their strength; they shall mount up with wings like eagles; they shall run and not be weary; they shall walk and not be faint"* (Isaiah 40:31). I mulled this over in my mind, and come morning, God reminded me again that He *is* in control. He is sovereign over all, even this horrendous situation we now find our family in. This is all in His hands. He will

Lessons in Farm Life

unfold *His* plan in *His* time and in *His* ways and I must not *presume* that he will grant my exact request unless it is a promise clearly stated in his word. I must be content to know that He *will work all things for the good of those who love him*. I was then filled with a peace and the faintest whisper of a song came back to me, and my heart was filled with praise and the song got louder until I felt as if I could almost burst with the song of praise that was in my heart.

I am so thankful that I can rest in the knowledge that my God is in control. There is no reason to get all stressed out, thinking I need to be doing something to change the situation. There is nothing we can say or do to change the heart of any individual, God must do that. The best thing we can do for our loved ones is to pray, pray that God will open their eyes to their need for Him and that he would break the chains of bondage that hold our loved ones in the grip of sin, *"..do not be anxious about anything, but in everything by prayer and supplication with thanksgiving let your requests be made known to God" (Philippians 4:6)*. We can also let them know that we love them no matter what and that we will always be there for them and we can encourage them to seek the Lord.

I think of how very different things might have been in our family right now, had I been the faithful example I should have been; but I do praise God that things aren't as bad as they could be. It is only by his sovereign grace that my husband and I stayed together all these years and are now blessed with a close and loving relationship. It is only

Showing His Sovereignty

by God's grace that our oldest son married such a fantastic young lady, whose desire is to serve the Lord. We are truly grateful for the daughter-in-law that God has blessed us with. I, myself am truly grateful for the husband that God blessed me with. Had my husband been unwilling to put up with the kind of wife I was for so many years- things would be drastically different within our family today. It is only by God's grace that he was able to hang in there- for I know I had caused him much hurt and pain throughout several years of our married life together. He was showing the unconditional love of Christ to his wife as an example of Christ's love for the Church throughout all that time. I was not displaying the submissive spirit toward my husband as I should have in order to display the submission we, as the Church, need to have toward our Lord. When we fail to follow God's instructions as to our roles within the marriage relationship- we not only create disharmony within the home, but we also distort the gospel by displaying an inaccurate portrayal of Christ's love for the Church, and how we should respond to that love through our submission to our Lord.

A famous ninteenth-century novelist by the name of Samuel Butler was once quoted as saying this in regards to Christ and the church: *"If He were to apply for a divorce on the grounds of cruelty, adultery and desertion, he would probably get one."* Mr. Butler's quote demonstrates an essential truth; the relationship between the Lord and His people is likened to a marriage, and the unfaithfulness we show to our Lord is as bad, or even worse, than a spouse's

Lessons in Farm Life

extramarital affair, *"Surely as a treacherous wife leaves her husband, so have you been treacherous to me, O house of Israel, declares the Lord" (Jeremiah 3:20).* This teaching is made particularly clear in the book of Hosea. It is here that we read the story of Hosea and Gomer: *"When the Lord first spoke through Hosea, the Lord said to Hosea, "Go, take to yourself a wife of whoredom and have children of whoredom, for the land commits great whoredom by forsaking the Lord" (Hosea 1:2).*

The Bible is as applicable to us today as it was back in the days of the Israelites. God hasn't changed and neither have his people. Many of those who profess to know Him are constantly turning their backs on our Lord and going after other gods. In going after these other gods, we are telling him we can make it on our own. Here we find just a few of many verses that exhort God's people to turn to him in repentance; *"Seek the Lord while he may be found, call upon him while he is near: Let the wicked forsake his way and the unrighteous man his thoughts: and let him return unto the Lord, and he will have mercy on him; and to our God, for he will abundantly pardon" (Isaiah 55:6-7). "Return, ye backsliding children, and I will heal your backslidings" (Jeremiah 3:22). "But this thing I commanded them, saying, 'Obey my voice, and I will be your God, and ye shall be my people; and walk ye in all the ways that I have commanded you, that it may be well unto you. But they hearkened not, nor inclined their ear, but walked in the counsels and in the imagination of their evil heart, and went backward, and not forward" (Jeremiah 7:23-24).* These portions of scripture

237

Showing His Sovereignty

should actually be read by chapter, not just by verses, for there is so much to gain from the reading of them.

If we are inclined to turning our backs on our Lord, we are actually breaking the first four commandments; 1) *"You shall have no other gods before me...."* 2) *"You shall not make for yourself a carved image.. or any likeness of anything... or serve them.."* 3) *"You shall not take the name of the Lord your God in vain, for the Lord will not hold him guiltless who takes his name in vain.."* 4) *"Remember the Sabbath day, to keep it holy," (Exodus 20:3-6).* I think we should make clear here that the definition of a carved image as defined in the dictionary is; to create an image of wood or stone, *or in one's mind.* So, we must not fool ourselves into thinking this commandment does not apply to us today just because we do not bow down to images that are visible, for an image can be as simple as an inaccurate portrayal of God within our own minds. So many people think of God as a great big buddy in the sky, or a Santa Claus figure; one who is jolly, loving and giving; a real pal. Well, God is not our 'pal'. He *is* loving and giving, but He is also a holy sovereign God who demands our complete allegiance. He is also a God of justice who hates sin, and does not turn a blind eye to sin. He *must* punish sin.

Let us be mindful that sin is *any* lack of conformity unto, or transgression of, the law of God. In other words, we not only sin through violation of scripture in doing wrong- we also sin by neglecting to follow God's commands in doing what is right. Considering the fact that our God is holy and demands perfection, that covers

Lessons in Farm Life

everything from our thoughts, to our attitudes, to our speech, to our actions. Just because we are not obvious sinners, ones who openly transgress God's laws in the ten commandments, does not mean that we are any less guilty in the sins that we do commit; those ones that we think are hidden or may be unaware of, such as pride, covetousness, envy, hatred, etc. Jesus makes very clear in Matthew that one who is even angry with his brother, is as liable to judgement as one who commits murder.

Our Lord showed more compassion for the harlots and adulterers than he did for the self- righteous Pharisees. These "pious" people did actually live a very moral lifestyle, but their hearts were far from God. We must be mindful not to condemn those who commit transgressions we would consider unthinkable, realizing we likely have sins within our own lives to deal with. We must examine our own hearts and minds in the light of scripture before we dare try to correct another person's transgression or sin. The good Lord just might need to open our eyes to some very grievous sins within our own hearts. If we are desirous to live holy and effective lives for Him, we must remember it is only by His grace that we are in that position.

In Psalm 89, we find God talking of David; *"If his children forsake my law and do not walk according to my rules, if they violate my statutes and do not keep my commandments, then I will punish their transgression with the rod and their iniquity with stripes, but I will not remove from him my steadfast love or be false to my faithfulness" (Psalm 89:30–33).*

Showing His Sovereignty

We must never presume upon God; taking for granted that just because we were born in a Christian home and have gone to church all our lives and have even been baptized and become a member of a church that God will go easy on us; that he will let us into heaven, if we are in fact not abiding in him. So many people out there who call themselves Christians have no idea what it really means to be a Christian. A Christian is one who actively seeks the help of the Holy Spirit as he/she lives a life that is preoccupied with his/her faith in God and the living out of that faith. We will see the evidence of this through one's life. They will show genuine love for all people, not just the ones within their family and their own little social circle. They will show their love for God in their service to others. They will strive to show others the gospel by seeking to fulfil the roles God has given them within their marriage relationships (if they are married); and in all other relationships they engage in.

We are so much like the Israelites of ages past. It is made very clear that God has allowed his people to go their own way by the evidence we see of so many broken relationships within 'Christian' circles, and so many 'professing Christian' kids abandoning the faith, "...*my people would not hearken to my voice;... So I gave them up unto their own heart's lust: and they walked in their own counsels. Oh that my people had hearkened unto me*" *(Psalm 81:11–13)*, "... *And I said to their children...Do not walk in the statutes of your fathers, nor keep their rules, nor defile yourselves with their idols... But the children rebelled against*

Lessons in Farm Life

me. They did not walk in my statutes and were not careful to obey my rules, by which, if a person does them, he shall live; they profaned my Sabbaths" (Ezekiel 20:18, 21). We must remember God's promise, "Draw near to God, and he will draw near to you .." (James 4:8). "For lo, they that are far from thee shall perish: thou hast destroyed all them that go a whoring from thee. But it is good for me to draw near to God: I have put my trust in the Lord God, that I may declare all thy works" (Psalm 73:27-28).

We are surrounded by many ungodly influences; so many temptations to sin, and when we neglect to look to the Holy Spirit for His enabling to overcome those temptations, praying that He would keep us on that right path that leads to righteousness, we will very easily be led off that path, "But each person is tempted when he is lured and enticed by his own desire. Then desire when it is conceived gives birth to sin, and sin when it is fully grown brings forth death" (James 1:14-15). If we do not avail ourselves of the instructions in God's Word; reading, studying, praying, listening to his Word, it will grow easier and easier for us to give in to those voices that are tempting us to sin. The Bible tells us one of the reasons for why we go through so much suffering, "My people are destroyed for lack of knowledge" (Hosea 4:6). The knowledge of God is to depart from evil. When we live without that knowledge of God, we will suffer the consequences of it, "As I entered into judgement with your fathers... so I will enter into judgement with you, declares the Lord God. I will make you pass under

Showing His Sovereignty

the rod, ... I will purge out the rebels from among you, and those who transgress against me" (Ezekiel 20: 36–38).

In the same way that we cannot gain access into heaven by our parents' profession, we also cannot blame our lethargic or inconsistent behavior on our parents- if they failed to live faithful consistent lives for the Lord. We all are responsible for our own actions. It is true outside influences do effect us. Two people can go through the same kind of trial and one may come out being drawn closer to God as a result and yet, the other may become bitter and turn away from God. If we are professing believers, we are responsible to be following God's instructions; if we are negligent in doing so, we will suffer the consequences of that negligence ourselves, (See Ezekiel chapter 18).

Thankfully, we have the hope and comfort of God's promises if we will turn our hearts toward him, God will give us sound teachers, *"..acknowledge your guilt, that you rebelled against the Lord your God and scattered your favors among foreigners under every green tree, and that you have not obeyed my voice, declares the Lord; for I am your master; I will take you,... and I will bring you to Zion. And I will give you shepherds after my own heart, who will feed you with knowledge and understanding" (Jeremiah 3: 13–15).* However, if we do not fully turn our hearts to God, He will give us teachers who will tell us only what we want to hear, *"For the time is coming when people will not endure sound teaching, but having itching ears they will accumulate for themselves teachers to suit their own passions, and will turn*

Lessons in Farm Life

away from listening to the truth and wander off into myths"(2 Timothy 4:3-4).

We must seek God diligently if we want to experience His blessing, *"As a pleasing aroma I will accept you, when I bring you out from the peoples, and gather you out of the countries where you have been scattered. And I will manifest my holiness among you in the sight of the nations. And you shall know that I am the Lord....... and you shall loathe yourselves for all the evils that you have committed. And you shall know that I am the Lord, when I deal with you for my name's sake, not according to your evil ways, nor according to your corrupt deeds...declares the Lord" (Ezekiel 20:41-44). "And I will betroth you to me forever. I will betroth you to me in righteousness and in justice, in steadfast love and in mercy. I will betroth you to me in faithfulness. And you shall know the Lord" (Hosea 2:19-20).* What a great and merciful God we serve, *"For thou, Lord, art good, and ready to forgive; and plenteous in mercy unto all them that call upon thee" (Psalm 86:5)!*

God **is** Sovereign, and if we can just get it into our heads that He truly is in control of *all* areas of our lives, then we can, by His grace, and with the help of His Holy Spirit live tremendously effective Christian lives for our Lord, *"I am God, and there is no other; I am God, and there is none like me...I say: My purpose will stand, and I will do all that I please... What I have said, that will I bring about; what I have planned, that will I do" (Isaiah 46:9-11).* God has a plan for each one of our lives, and He is working out that plan throughout each and every day that we live, and

243

Showing His Sovereignty

if we can trust that He is, by His providence, working all things for our good, we will be looking to Him to guide our every step, *"And we know for those who love God all things work together for good, for those who are called according to his purpose" (Romans 8:28).* I would prefer a translation that would say God is working *through* all things for our good, for the things themselves are definitely *not* good. When a family loses a home to fire, or parents suffer the loss of a beloved child, or the heartache of a wayward child...., those things in and of themselves are *not* good. However, God will work *through* those things *for* our good, to teach us the lessons he wants us to learn and to draw us closer to him.

I do not believe that it is merely a coincidence that I started this book back in February of the year 2011, a few months after we had started to pray more fervently for the work of God's grace within the lives of our families. I began this book with the intention of relating to my family what a difference the work of the Holy Spirit had made within my life. And I do not believe it is merely a coincidence that I had sent what I thought were all of my stories off to the dear couple who suggested I write a book to begin with, for editing purposes at that time, thinking I was ready to pull it all together into book form. Neither do I believe it to be merely coincidental that the major drastic and devastating events that occurred within our family had taken place at just such a time as to prompt me to allude to them in these last few sections of this book that I started over four years ago. It is also no coincidence

244

Lessons in Farm Life

that, in God's timing and providence the publication of this book was delayed for over three years, (and that it has even been at the publisher's for over one year). I have been so thankful that it was not printed for the public back when I thought it was ready, as I have made numerous changes since that time- right up until the last time I had our son send it in to be printed (and even one more time after that). God is Sovereign and in complete control. All things will happen according to His plan and in His timing. I am so thankful He is in complete control over every area of our lives and of our loved ones' as well, regardless of the circumstances we may be dealing with.

It is always such a sad experience within a family when marriages fall apart. Many times we do not even suspect that there may be a problem within the marriage of ones we think we know so well. Yet, there have been many 'professing Christians' who have parted ways. One spouse may have left the other, or they may have come to a mutual agreement to separate, or divorce the one they vowed before God and others to stick with through good times and bad, for rich or for poor, for better or worse- till death should part them.

It is with much sorrow that we hear of such marriages falling apart time and again. However, we must also realize that we ourselves may be guilty of not keeping our own marriage vows toward our spouse in the way that we should, even if we have not actually separated or divorced. We fail in this every time we get angry toward one another, every time we argue to get our own way, every time we

Showing His Sovereignty

actually put our own needs and desires ahead of those of our spouse. When we do these things we are breaking the vow to love the other till death part us. Getting angry, arguing for one's own way, and covetousness are all signs of selfishness- not love for another. Any time we fail to live up to our profession of faith according to Christ's teaching, we are failing to show a true love for our spouse. If we really want to know if we are truly fulfilling our marriage vows in loving our spouse as we should, we need to read 1 Corinthians 13 and then ask ourselves; "Am I showing this kind of love to my spouse"?

The Bible tells us the greatest commandment is to love the Lord your God with all your heart, mind and soul, and to love your neighbor (we could substitute spouse, or anyone else for neighbor,) as yourself. How many of us can truly say that we have even followed this command for one day? Jesus says, *"If you love me, you will keep my commandments,"* (John 14:15). Do we desire to study his Word so that we can keep his commandments and thereby show our love for him; Or are we far too absorbed in meeting our own selfish desires? It is indeed high time that we, who call ourselves Christians, start to really live as if we *are* ones who follow after Christ.

Perhaps we are in need of turning our hearts back to the Lord in repentance for the lethargic way we have been serving Him. We must not be trying to serve Him through our own efforts alone, but totally surrender our all to Him, seeking His enabling grace. Only then can we be ready and waiting to expect His blessing; for God *will* bless us greatly

Lessons in Farm Life

when we truly show a desire to live for Him, *"Blessed be the God and Father of our Lord Jesus Christ, who hath blessed us with all spiritual blessings in heavenly places in Christ: According as he hath chosen us in him before the foundation of the world, that we should be holy and without blame before him in love"* (Ephesians 1:3–4).

We must recognize that God is Sovereign and He *is* in control! Our God is in complete control over every major circumstance within our lives; as evidenced in Jesus' calming of the sea when in the boat with His disciples; *"And a windstorm came down on the lake, and they were filling with water and were in danger. And they went and woke him, saying, "Master, master, we are perishing!" And he awoke and rebuked the wind and the raging waves, and they ceased, and there was a calm"* (Luke 8:23-24).

Our God is also in control over every minor circumstance within our lives, as evidenced in Matthew; *"But even the hairs of your head are all numbered"* (Matthew 10:30). Nothing escapes his notice, *"Are not two sparrows sold for a penny? And not one of them will fall to the ground apart from your Father...(verse 29)* Not meaning that they are falling to their death, but that they are merely lighting on the ground, and the use of the words, "apart from your Father," would indicate that God is truly Sovereign over all activities of beasts, even the smallest sparrow that flies in the sky.

There is nothing so small within our lives as to be insignificant to our God. He truly is in complete control over all. When we come to surrender our all to his

Showing His Sovereignty

providential care, we will truly experience a freedom from the bondage to so many sins, and a joy in living, as we look to God for his enabling grace to get us through each and every day. Let us be marvellously aware of the goodness, mercy and grace of our Lord and Savior, as He shows us His Sovereignty.

21

Come to the Call...

2 Corinthians 5:20-21

This story comes in contrast to the the one relating to the tale of my obliging bossy, Annabelle. Contrary to the cooperative cow found in Annabelle's story, this is a tale of a not so obliging bossy. It also took place several years ago, at the Lakeville farm. However, I do not have any such feelings of pride associated with this cow, rather more pangs of regret and remorse. This cow went by the name of Doreen. I did *not* name this cow. I would never name a cow Doreen. I always favored such names as Anna-belle, May-belle and Mari-belle. They just seemed to have a nice ring to them, (no pun intended). Anyway, to get back to Doreen, she was a purebred registered Scottish Highland cow. We bought her from a German couple who raised

Come to the Call...

Highlanders just down the road from us. If you've never seen a Scottish Highlander before, you can recognize them by their long shaggy fur and wide curving horns. Their bodies are quite stocky with short legs. They also have short stubby noses and are usually a brown, blond, or reddish color. Purebred black Highlanders are rare. Doreen happened to be a reddish colored beast and she really was quite handsome. Too bad she hadn't come with a more impressive cow-like name. I will always remember the day my husband brought her home. She was in an enclosed trailer and before it even stopped moving I could hear the thumping and crashing within. I was anxious for him to let her out and get her safely into the pasture. I guess she was just as anxious to be out, for as soon as the trailer stopped she came crashing out over the back door. I had no idea cows could jump so high. Unfortunately for us, this farm was located fairly close to the road, so of course that was exactly where the limb footed Doreen headed, and the chase was on. It was hard to imagine that such a short- legged shaggy beast could run so fast, let alone jump so high.

Since we lived in a small village on this farm the scene that followed was enjoyed by more than one or two curious neighbors. One of them even joined in the chase. I apologized for the inconvenience. He informed me there was no need, for this was the most excitement he'd had in years. He was really enjoying himself. I was not entirely happy to oblige him in the pleasure he derived from chasing our cow through the village streets, for I was

Lessons in Farm Life

quite confident in feeling that this cow would not be one to come at the sound of my call. In fact this cow did not even spend one year with us on the Lakeville Farm as she came to an early demise. I'm afraid if you are curious to hear of her misfortune you will have to be disappointed as that is one story I'd much sooner forget. Sufficient to say had she been of my obliging bossy, Annabelle's, nature, and learned to come to the sound of my call, she might very well have been with us yet.

Musing over the contrast between these two beasts, one so obliging and willing to come to the call of her master's voice and the other so contrary and rebellious, instead of coming to the call of her name- she was more inclined to run in the opposite direction- made me think of the comparison in the Bible of sheep to Christians who know the sound of their master's voice and follow it, "... *we are his people and the sheep of his pasture" (Psalm 100:3).* *"...the sheep hear his voice, and he calls his own sheep by name and leads them out" (John 10:3).* He is our Shepherd, we are His sheep.

This analogy also brings to mind the very familiar and comforting Psalm of David. In Psalm 23 we find, *"The Lord is my Shepherd; I shall not want."* I never really understood that first phrase as a young child, always tending to run it all into one sentence which didn't really make sense. Of course it makes total sense when you understand the division between the words Shepherd and I. Do we really understand that little phrase, 'I shall not want'? The image of our Lord as a shepherd here is as

251

Come to the Call...

one who stays with his flock, *"He will tend His flock like a shepherd" (Isaiah 40:11)*. Sheep are totally dependent upon the shepherd for all of their needs. They are dependent on him for food, water and protection from wild animals. We also are totally dependent on our Shepherd for all of our needs. We will not want for anything. Do we ever stop and consider how very dependent we are on God? We are dependent on Him for every single need that we have and He supplies each and every one, *"And my God shall supply every need of yours according to His riches in glory in Christ Jesus" (Philippians 4:19)*. He gives us the very air that we breathe. Without it we would die, *"Thus says God, the Lord, who created the heavens and stretched them out, who spread out the earth and what comes from it, who gives breath to the people on it and spirit to those who walk in it" (Isaiah 42:5)*.

He provides us with food and clothing, *"Look at the birds of the air: they neither sow nor reap nor gather into barns, and yet your heavenly Father feeds them. Are you not of more value than they?" ... But if God so clothes the grass of the field, which today is alive and tomorrow is thrown into the oven, will he not much more clothe you, O you of little faith? Therefore do not be anxious, saying, 'What shall we eat?' Or 'What shall we drink?' Or 'What shall we wear?' ...For your heavenly Father knows that you need them all. But seek first the kingdom of God and his righteousness, and all these things will be added to you" (Matthew 6: 26, 30-33)*. I think we need to pay careful attention to that last line, ***"But seek first the kingdom of God and his righteousness, and all these things will be added unto you."*** We cannot expect God to

Lessons in Farm Life

meet all of our needs if we do not have our priorities in the right order, (2 Thessalonians 3:10).

Not only does He give us physical life, but He also gives us spiritual life through the gift of His Holy Spirit, *"It is the Spirit who gives life; the flesh is no help at all. The words that I have spoken to you are spirit and life" (John 6:63).* If we are ones who are filled with the Spirit, our focus will be on the things of the Lord; *"For those who live according to the flesh set their minds on the things of the flesh, but those who live according to the Spirit set their minds on the things of the Spirit" (Romans 8:5).* Our desire will be to do the work of the Kingdom.

He lay down His own life for the sins of His people, *"I am the Good Shepherd. I know my own and my own know me, just as the Father knows me and I know the Father; and I lay down my life for the sheep" (John 10:14-15). "He Himself bore our sins in His body on the tree, that we might die to sin and live to righteousness. By His wounds you have been healed. For you were straying like sheep, but have now returned to the Shepherd and Overseer of your souls" (1 Peter 2:24-25).* He holds us in the palm of his hand, *"My sheep hear my voice, and I know them, and they follow me. I give them eternal life, and they will never perish, and no one will snatch them out of my hand. My Father, who has given them to me, is greater than all, and no one is able to snatch them out of the Father's hand. I and the Father are one" (John 10:27-30).* What a wonderful comfort to know that those He has called into the fold, are His forever. We need never worry that He will ever leave us completely on our own.

Come to the Call...

He is our Shepherd; the Good Shepherd who lovingly looks after His flock, *"For I am persuaded that neither death, nor life, nor angels, nor principalities, nor powers, nor things present, nor things to come. Nor height, nor depth, nor any other creature, shall be able to separate us from the love of God, which is in Christ Jesus our Lord" (Romans 8:38-39).*

Not only does our Shepherd help to meet our physical needs, He also provides us with all that we need spiritually as well. He does this through the teaching of His word, *"Let the word of Christ dwell in you richly, teaching and admonishing one another in all wisdom ..." (Colossians 3:16). "Behold, you delight in truth in the inward being, and you teach me wisdom in the secret heart" (Psalm 51:6).*

Because of the existence of hostile spiritual powers, our duty as Christians to live pure lives for the sake of the Gospel is a difficult task. We are encouraged however, to face these evil hosts in Christ's strength and not in our own. As we are conformed more and more to the image of Christ, we gain confidence in resisting the devil's temptations; For we have confidence in knowing that Christ has had the victory over all temptation, *"For because he Himself has suffered when tempted, he is able to help those who are being tempted" (Hebrews 2:18). "For we do not have a high priest who is unable to sympathize with our weaknesses, but one who in every respect has been tempted as we are, yet without sin" (Hebrews 4:15).*

If we are truly His and should go astray, we can be assured that He will bring us back, *"I have gone astray like a lost sheep; seek your servant, for I do not forget your*

Lessons in Farm Life

commandments" *(Psalm 119:176).* Let us remember that we have the promise in His word that whatsoever we ask according to His will, we will receive; *"And this is the confidence that we have toward him, that if we ask anything according to his will he hears us. And if we know that he hears us in whatever we ask, we know that we have the requests that we have asked of him" (1 John 5:14-15).* What a wonderful promise. If we, who are truly in Christ, find ourselves, or another Christian, straying off the path, rebelling, and even running from God; we can know that He will bring this wayward sheep back into the fold. He **will** do it, for He has promised, *"For thus says the Lord God. Behold, I, **I myself will search for my sheep and will seek them out.** As a shepherd seeks out his flock when he is among his sheep that have been scattered so will I seek out my sheep, and **I will rescue them from all places where they have been scattered** on a day of clouds and thick darkness." "I will seek the lost, and I will bring back the strayed, and I will bind up the injured, and I will strengthen the weak, ..."(Ezekiel 34:11-12, 16).*

We take great comfort in God's wonderful promises as we continue to pray for His work of grace to be done in the lives of our loved ones. Circumstances have still not changed for the better within our family, however, we continue to pray in faith, believing that God will work through these circumstances for our good and His glory. We have great hopes that He will bring about much healing and reconciling of relationships, not only within our own family, but also in many others that we have been

255

Come to the Call...

praying for as well. We cannot presume upon God and say we are 100% certain that He will do as we desire, for we do not know the mind of God. However, it would seem good to us for Him to bring about much restoration in so many areas. Unless He shows us clearly this is not His plan, we will continue to pray for reconciliation to take place. We have the utmost of confidence that our God will do what is right; for the good of his people and in order to bring glory to His most Holy name.

This past week I have been impressed with the fact of how God uses us to accomplish His purposes. We are ambassadors for Christ, put here on this earth to serve Him by our service to others, *"Therefore we are ambassadors for Christ, God making his appeal through us. We implore you on behalf of Christ, be reconciled to God" (2 Corinthians 5:20-21).* He is using us to reach out to the lost, the straying, the injured and the weak. What a tremendous privilege and responsibility He has granted to us. Let us not shrink back from the enormity of this task, even though it may very well mean that we will need to go through many hardships and much pain. Thankfully, we can be filled with His power and peace- as we look to our Lord for his strength and enabling grace in undertaking this tremendous responsibility.

Here we find Paul speaking to us from God's Word, having endured many hardships for the sake of the Gospel; *"We put no obstacle in anyone's way, so that no fault may be found in our ministry, but as servants of God we commend ourselves in every way: by great endurance, in afflictions,*

Lessons in Farm Life

hardships, calamities, beatings, imprisonments, riots, labors, sleepless nights, hunger; by purity, knowledge, patience, kindness, the Holy Spirit, genuine love; by truthful speech, and the power of God; with the weapons of righteousness for the right hand and for the left; through honor and dishonor, through slander and praise. We are treated as impostors, and yet are true: as unknown, and yet well known; as dying, and behold, we live; as punished, and yet not killed; as sorrowful, yet always rejoicing; as poor, yet making many rich; as having nothing, yet possessing everything. We have spoken freely to you, Corinthians; our heart is wide open. You are not restricted by us, but you are restricted in your own affections" (2 Corinthians 6:3-12).

The passage from Ezekiel quoted above, where he refers to God as our Shepherd, bringing us back into the fold, puts us in mind of the parable of the lost sheep found in Matthew 18:12-14, *"What do you think? If a man has a hundred sheep and one of them has gone astray, does he not leave the ninety-nine on the mountains and go in search of the one that went astray? And if he finds it, truly, I say to you, he rejoices more than over the ninety-nine that never went astray. So it is not the will of my Father who is in heaven that one of these little ones should perish."* This is a clear indication of God's preservation for not only His Church (made up of those regenerate members all over the globe and within various denominations), but for each individual within the Church. It shows us His commitment to each disciple and in particular, His care for those who have gone astray and are in danger. If you are hearing the call of

257

Come to the Call...

the Shepherd, won't you answer? Come to the call of your Heavenly Father, and be prepared to expect an abundance of blessing in so doing. What a wonderful sense of peace and comfort is ours in the knowledge that we are under the protective care of our Great Shepherd, the keeper of our souls.

Autobiographical Note

I had made a 'decision' to follow Christ at an early age and lived a fairly consistent moral lifestyle. Having always been very active in church activities from the time I was quite young, I thought I was a fairly good 'Christian'. I even married a nice Christian fellow, a very nice Christian fellow, actually. However, what I failed to understand at that time was that in order to be a true follower of Christ, I couldn't live an effective Christian life in my own strength. I needed to be daily crucifying self and seeking the enabling of the Holy Spirit to guide me in my daily life. Unless I learned to walk in step with the Holy Spirit, I would be helpless in making the kind of choices and decisions that would be honoring to my Lord. I had to learn to deny myself, and that was one of many things I just had not learned to do. However, I was due to experience some major 'lessons in life'.

Early on in our marriage, my husband had expressed to me his interest in being involved in Christian ministry. He was really quite keen on heading off to some foreign land as a missionary. I, however, was not at all enthused with this idea. Going off to an unknown land full of

259

strangers and poisonous creatures did not appeal to me in the least, so I was not at all supportive of his idea. My concerns lay more with building a home and raising a family. My focus was more on pleasing me, and my husband's focus was on pleasing God. It is no wonder our marriage was not as harmonious as it should have been for so many years. As a 'Christian' couple, we *both* needed to be focused on living to please God. If I had worked more on my relationship with God at the beginning of our marriage, I know things would have been closer to the way they should have been in our homelife. Our marriage as Christians should be like a three sided triangle with God at the peak. If each spouse (situated in the other two bottom angles) endeavors to grow closer in their relationship to God first and foremost, the closer they grow to Him, the closer they are bound to grow in their relationship to one another as well.

My poor husband did actually give up on his missionary aspirations, due mostly to my lack of support, but also in lieu of his increased involvement with work and then as time wore on, family responsibilities. I can really understand why Paul said that he who refrains from marriage does better than the one who marries. It really is true that the married man is anxious about worldly things, how to please his wife, and so his interests are divided. Yet the unmarried man is more concerned with the things of the Lord and how to please Him. The same goes for the married and unmarried woman, though I would have to ashamedly admit that I was more concerned with pleasing myself than pleasing my husband.

I was very self-centered, very much focused on 'me'. I'm sure my family would not have failed to notice that I had actually been a rather bitter and discontented 'professing Christian' for several years. The reason for my discontentment, *(I believed) to be caused by financial stress. Finances never bothered my husband, however. He would say the Lord had always provided him with all that he needed in the past, and he was confident that He would continue to do so. Even when we were in way over our heads due to business failure at the beginning of our marriage, he was very calm and confident that God would supply the money that was needed to pay the bills. Of course, he was always right, the money did come, and sometimes just when we needed it, even though we never let on to anyone that we were really very strapped financially for a period of time. *I have come to realize in recent years that the main reason for my discontentment was (ultimately) *not* due to a lack of finances, but more to the fact that, as a 'professing Christian', I was not in a right relationship with God. I am so thankful for the work of grace that God has done in my life these past several years.

It has actually been six years since the time of my conversion. Of course God had been working within my life prior to this, however, the changes that took place at that time were more evident within my heart, giving me a real desire to apply biblical truths to the way that I live. It has not been, and isn't an easy transition, as God continues to work in my life. In fact this sanctification process can be very slow and painful. I am so thankful for the many truths that God has revealed, (and continues to reveal) to me through His word by His Spirit. I am so thankful that God is helping me to change the focus of my life, taking it off of 'me' and putting it where it belongs, on Him. I'm afraid my poor family had to put up with an awful lot before God did that transforming work of grace within my heart and life, causing me to see my need to deny myself, and look to the enabling of the Holy Spirit to lead and guide me in the way He would have me to go- rather than following my own (focussed- on- self) pathway. Unfortunately, our older children were already out of the house by this time. I don't want for people to think that I was *that* terrible most of the time. However, there were many times, when things didn't go my way, that I did not even attempt to make life very pleasant for my family. I could be a very 'moody mother'. I could be a very angry mother and I was a very discontented wife and mother, finding myself to be of a negative and complaining attitude much of the time as certain circumstances within our lives continued to remain unchanged.

I recall asking my husband one night, quite some time ago, how he could love me, for I considered myself to be very unlovable at the time I made this inquiry. God had been revealing to me many areas in my life that needed to change and I was feeling overwhelmed by my past failures; the many sins that I had been blind to for so long. I knew that I had caused my spouse much pain due to my many years of dealing with anger, discontentment, bitterness and resentment. I remember very clearly the answer he gave me to my question of how he could love me. As he held me in his arms, he said to me in such a tender voice, "Christ gives me this love I have for you"…. I can't even begin to express the gratitude I have to God for blessing me with a husband that faithfully obeyed God's command to love his wife unconditionally as Christ loves his bride, the Church. I just wish I would have been the faithful wife I should have been, submitting to and respecting my husband as a clear example of how we, as the church, are to submit to Christ. I know our lives would be very different today had I determined to be obedient to scripture's teaching in regard to my role as wife and mother. They would be different not only materially, which is not so important, but they would be far different in other ways as well, more important and eternally significant ways.

Had I been striving to be the obedient wife as outlined in God's word that I should have been years ago, displaying to my children a faithful Christian witness, I'm certain we would not have gone through nearly so many struggles and heartaches in the raising of our family. Had I loved my children unconditionally, taken the time to really sit down and have heart to heart talks with them, focusing on the importance of disciplining them in the ways of the Lord, I know we would be a much closer and more loving family today.

I am thankful however, that even though I understand how responsible I am for my past failures (that truly do grieve me greatly), I can take comfort in knowing that all that has happened in my life and in the lives of our family has been according to God's providence. There is a reason for all that has happened within our lives- good or bad, and God will work through all of those circumstances to bring about good for those of us who love Him and for His glory. We do need to understand how very important it is that we strive to be godly role models for our children, showing them faithful examples of how a true follower of Christ should live in every area of life on a daily, (moment by moment even) basis. It is also very important that we point them to God's Word and pray that the Holy Spirit would lead and guide them in the truth of it.

I have learned how very different life can be when one determines not to focus on oneself. If we are more concerned with the needs of those around us, we don't have time to worry over every little thing connected with 'me'. When we come to realize that we serve a Sovereign God who is in complete control over every area of our lives and is working all things for our good, we are left with absolutely no reason to worry. That doesn't mean that we won't worry, but that we shouldn't. It is only human to have cares and concerns, or even burdens at times; However, we also have a Heavenly Father who knows our every need, who we can go to at any time and share those troubles with. He will either take those burdens away or he will give us the grace to bear them. He can take away our fears and leave us with a peace; a peace that only He can give, but we must be looking to Him to do this.

Instead of being discontented with various aspects of our lives, we must be seeking our Lord diligently- being always on the look-out for ways that we can serve Him. When we are obedient to his word, He will help us to realize how very blessed we are with what we have and remind us that we are to be living on this earth with the knowledge that our stay here is very temporary; that we can look forward to a much better life in heaven with our Lord and Savior for all of eternity. How different all of our lives could be if we would live with an all- pervading sense of God's presence, focusing on our need to be living in such a way so as to bring glory to our Holy God, each and every day and in all that we do.

I know I can't go back and change any of my past mistakes; However, I am thankful for the many lessons God has taught me through those many errors. I am also confident that I can, by God's grace, go on to live a faithful life striving to obey God's commands and encouraging my family to do the same. I can, also by God's grace, strive to be the godly role model to my grandchildren that I need to be and encourage their parents to pay careful attention to God's commands to nurture and train their children in the ways of the Lord. The most important thing I do is to pray (fervently) that God, by his Spirit, would do a mighty work in each one of our lives, that He would give each one of us a continuing hunger for His word and a desire to have a better understanding of who He is, and of our responsibility toward our Holy God. My wish is that each member of our family would give evidence of a desire to live holy lives that are pleasing to our Lord; that we would all live in such a way as to prompt others to ask us of the reason of the hope that we have within us, and that we would truly praise, honor and give glory to our great God and Savior, Jesus Christ our Lord.

List of Books for
Recommended Reading

the <u>Holy Bible</u>- inspired by God, (2 Peter 1:19-21; 2 Timothy 3:16-17)

Helpful aids:

<u>The Sovereignty of God</u> by Arthur W. Pink

<u>The Cost of Discipleship</u> by Dietrich Bonhoeffer

<u>At the Throne of Grace</u> by John MacArthur

<u>Building a Godly Home</u> by William Gouche

<u>The Sermon on the Mount</u> by Sinclair Ferguson

<u>This Momentary Marriage</u> by John Piper

<u>The Excellent Wife</u> by Martha Peace

<u>A Tale of Two Sons</u> by John MacArthur

<u>Resisting Gossip</u> by Matthew C. Mitchell

<u>Renewing Your Mind in a Mindless World </u>by James
Montgomery Boice

<u>Blame it on the Brain </u>by Edward T. Welch

I'm sure there are many more excellent books by Christian
writers out there that would be very helpful guides in our
Christian living. These are just ones I have come across and
found very helpful in more recent years.(I actually have
not read <u>Building a Godly Home </u>by William Gouche.
However, it is on my list of books to order as I did listen
to an excellent series of talks given by various speakers
using material gleaned from William Gouche's book.)
We need also to keep in mind that we should not accept
for truth everything we read just because it is written by
a Christian, no matter how well known or well educated
that person may be. Everything we read should be filtered
through the true teaching of scripture, as revealed by
the Holy Spirit. **God's Holy Word must be our ultimate
guide and source of truth for right living.**

Postscript

Due to finding out a close family member had been sexually abused for several years, I would like to add the following note of encouragement to any and all who may find themselves involved in a similar situation.

Note to children or adults who are victims of abuse:
Knowing of the years of pain and struggling that more than one family member has gone through having experienced this kind of heartache, I would strongly encourage you to confide in someone you can trust. Do not keep your past or present abuse a secret. The longer things are kept quiet, the more people that may become involved. You need to understand if you are a victim of this person, you are likely not the only one. You need help and the person victimizing you needs help. Many abusers have been victims of abuse themselves. Both parties are in need of help and healing. Please, tell a friend or family member, anyone you know you can trust who will want to help you. I plead with you- *Please* help stop this cycle of hurt. You need also understand that the most important thing you can do is to seek God diligently. He is the only

one who can ultimately bring healing from your past or present circumstances.

Note to parents:

While it is true we live in a scary world, it is also true that our God is sovereign over all things. He knows where we are, He knows what we are going through, and He is always working out His purpose in our lives to bring about the healing that needs to occur. We need not live in fear of today, tomorrow or even our past or the past of our children. He has a purpose and a plan for all that occurs within the lives of His people. Even though we may not understand why God would permit such pain to occur in the lives of His children, if we truly love Him, we must trust that He will work through all things for our good, even those things that in and of themselves may be very painful or even very evil.

A very helpful verse God has been impressing on my heart in recent days has been the one found in *Matthew 6:34;* *"Take therefore no thought for the morrow: for the morrow shall take thought for the things of itself. Sufficient unto the day is the evil thereof."* In other words, take one day at a time. We all have enough troubles to deal with in the day we are in. He has told us not to worry about tomorrow, don't even think about what troubles you may have to face in the days to come. We need to be seeking God and His enabling grace with each new day. When Paul pleaded with the Lord to remove his affliction, our Lord's response was; *"My grace is sufficient for you, for my power is made perfect in weakness"* (2 Corinthians 12:9). That is truly all we need to get us through each passing day- God's- marvellous- grace. When others witness God's strength evident in such weak and imperfect people- what a testimony that will be to the power of God at work.

When we truly understand that God is in control over everything, *every* little thing, there is such a peace in that even in the midst of the heavy storms in our lives. We can know and be assured that even if everything isn't made right here on this earth and in our time, it will all be made right one day- when we shall see Him as He is and He will wipe away every tear from our eyes *"...weeping may endure for a night, but joy comes in the morning"* (Psalm 30:5).

The following resources for those in need of help as well as to those who wish to be a support to a loved one in need of help can be ordered online through Amazon.

The Wounded Heart by Dr. Dan B. Allender

Dr. Allender has an excellent reputation, having received his M. Div. From Westminster Theological Seminary. He is a professor of counselling at The Seattle School of Theology and Psychology in Seattle Washington.

On the Threshold of Hope by Diane Langberg; and Bringing Abused Women to Christ ; also by Diane Langberg

Diane Langberg also has an excellent reputation and has been involved in counselling for several decades. She is a teacher at Westminster Seminary, Philadelphia. For more information you can check out this link; http://www.dianelangberg.com/work/diane.html

My final words to any and all who this last page may apply to:

May God be with you and may He use the circumstances of your life to either bring you into a right relationship with Himself, or to strengthen the relationship you now enjoy with the only One who can bring peace and healing through all of the brokenness and pain of this earthly life. May He shine his face upon us and grant us all his marvellous peace.

In Christ's great and amazing love,
Nancy Graham

CPSIA information can be obtained at www.ICGtesting.com
Printed in the USA
BVOW08s0541030915

415952BV00001B/2/P